Learn to Accept Yourself and Understand Others

Handbook for Emotional, Physical, and Spiritual Wellness

Esther White

Learn to Accept Yourself and Understand Others
Handbook for Emotional, Physical, and Spiritual Wellness

iUniverse books may be ordered through booksellers or by contacting:

iUniverse
1663 Liberty Drive
Bloomington, IN 47403
www.iuniverse.com
1-800-Authors (1-800-288-4677)

ISBN: 978-1-4697-5003-3 (sc)
ISBN: 978-1-4697-5005-7 (hc)
ISBN: 978-1-4697-5004-0 (e)

Printed in the United States of America

iUniverse rev. date: 10/07/2014

.*Appreciation Page*

For my daughter, Diane Christian, who has been the listening board for my ideas and fears, as well as being a constant source of good advice and encouragement.

For Mrs. Karen Phair, Home Economics teacher at our local high school for seeing the value of the information within these pages and sharing it with her students.

For the people who have attended the seminars and expressed Their appreciation for the positive impact the information has made in their lives.

Dedicated to
My husband, Bob, who has endured being alone while I have been at my computer and has been a faithful and steady companion as he promised many years ago.

Artwork by:
Alan Hutchinson
40 Jackson Lane
Jay, ME 04239
Telephone 207-645-2768, Cell Phone 207-491-9282
e-mail: alanh7@localnet.com

Table of Contents

Introduction

It all started when my husband and I attended a Marriage Enrichment Seminar, which introduced us to the Four Basic Temperament Theory.

At first I was devastated with the results of my evaluation. The word "despair" had a new and more vivid meaning to me than ever before. The more I looked at the results, I began to focus on the strengths I have instead of my weaknesses. Then my experience turned from despair to a better appreciation of who I am than I had ever had experienced before.

I decided to put what I had learned in a teaching format for our own children in our home school. I gave a copy to the local high guidance counselor to see if it would meet the school's guidelines as a health course. After he read the course, he asked if I would present it to the evening adult classes offered by our school district. From there it has grown into a compilation of nine sessions and this book.

I find it very rewarding to have class attendees tell me how their lives have changed by the information I have shared with them.

One of those great moments in life was when my granddaughter, soon to graduate from high school, dropped by to visit one day. She noticed the prototype of this book lying on my desk. She showed interest in it and said, "Gram, this is what I learned in school this year." I asked her if she liked it. Her response was, "It was the best class I had all through high school." perked my interest. When I asked her why she felt that way, she quickly responded, "Because it was something I could use in life."

Her response warmed my heart and spurred me on to complete this book and to make the information available to more people.

Learn To
Accept Yourself
&
Understand Others©

This book was written because we are becoming a society of drug users, alcoholics, physical and mental abusers, sports and media addicts and in a variety of other ways that causes problems for society and ourselves. The goal is to help people accept and appreciate who they are and to become more tolerant of others as well. This is an exciting study of the part of our inherited personality known as the Four Basic Temperament Theory.

There is a need for such an education. We have marriages and families falling apart. Parents and children often do not get along with each other. Misunderstandings run rampant at all levels of society. Knowing this subject can be a very useful tool in understanding who we are and why we differ from each other.

If three generations of your aunts and uncles had curly hair and skied the Matterhorn, chances are that you're a curly-haired athlete, too. And, yes, personality gets passed on as well. The Temperament Theory has been acclaimed by many as the best explanation of human behavior available.

Though an understanding of the temperaments is not a cure-all for every problem, it can be a tremendous help to many by raising self-esteem and improving relationships. When fully understood the Temperament Theory is a useful tool to understand, appreciate and celebrate our differences.

The Temperament Theory will be compared to and combined with other proven studies throughout the following pages.

This theory was first named and defined by the Greek physician, Hippocrates in 460-370 B.C. As a result of his observations, he distinguished four temperaments: Sanguine, Choleric, Melancholic, and Phlegmatic. He proposed that a person's temperament depended, on the 'humors' or bodily fluids: blood, yellow bile, black bile, and phlegm.

Though his theory of humors was debunked, his observations regarding the Four Basic temperaments proved to be very accurate indeed. It is the basis of many testing performed in institutes of learning to determine a person's vocational aptitude.

1. *The Four Basic Temperament Theory, http://psy.rin.ru/eng/article/147-101.html*

In 1798, German philosopher Immanuel Kant revived interest in the theory. Others since then have given brief descriptions, but Dr. Hales, in 1962, published a comprehensive and significant study. Dr.Tim LaHaye, Florence Litteaur and others have also written many books about the temperament theory. This theory is currently being used widely in the fields of education and business.

What you have in your hands is a compilation of eight seminars making the information available in one place for people to read at their own leisure. The Temperament Square is used throughout the various chapters.

Explanation of the Temperament Square

Left Side Emotional		**Right Side** Unemotional	
Top Half, Extroverts			
Picture	Temperament Word Description	Picture	Temperament Word Description
STRENGTHS	WEAKNESSES	STRENGTHS	WEAKNESSES
Bottom Half, Introverts			
Picture	Temperament Word Description	Picture	Temperament Word Description
STRENGTHS	WEAKNESSES	STRENGTHS	WEAKNESSES

Overview of the Temperament Theory
(The inherited part of the personality)

Temperament differs from personality but is part of the total personality. The rest of the personality comes from our culture, background, and environment. Both temperament and the rest of the personality influence a person's character.

The total personality is made up of more than just our temperament. It is made up of our inherited temperament plus other factors such as:

Childhood Training
Age
Sex
Environment
Education
Physical condition
Spiritual condition
Emotional condition

There is no best temperament. Each Temperament has strengths and weaknesses.

No one has just one temperament. We are all blends of the four basic temperaments.

⟹ It is unusual to test out high in just one area. If you do, you are referred to as being, "Super."

⟹ Usually people score highest in two areas, sometimes three.

⟹ The best way to explain the temperaments is to describe the four basic ones.

⟹ You will have more of the characteristics in the areas that you scored the highest number in.

⟹ If you score about the same in all four areas, you are what would be considered, "well rounded." It will be more difficult for you to see yourself in any particular section of the temperament square.

⟹ There can be modifications in our temperament due to various factors; but, our basic temperament remains the same.

Example of the Four Basic Temperaments Square

To determine your temperament: Before reading any further, underline or highlight the words in each category you feel are descriptive of you under the STRENGTHS and WEAKNESSES column.

Sanguine
The Talker
(BOLD)

Choleric
The Accomplisher
(BOLD)

STRENGTHS	WEAKNESSES	STRENGTHS	WEAKNESSES
Outgoing	Talker	Born Leader	Bossy
Story Teller	Exaggerates	Bold	Work-a-holic
Lives-in-Present	Disorganized	Dynamic	Slave Driver
Optimistic	Forgetful	Optimistic	Inconsiderate
Friendly	Unfocused	Organized	Opinionated
Carefree	Loud	Decisive	Sarcastic
Responsive	Egotistical	Goal oriented	Loud
		Enjoys working	

Melancholy
Detail Conscious
(FEARFUL)

Phlegmatic
The Watcher
(FEARFUL)

STRENGTHS	WEAKNESSES	STRENGTHS	WEAKNESSES
Sensitive	Unsociable	Quiet	Unenthusiastic
Perfectionist	Rigid standards	Relaxed	Stubborn
Quiet	Moody	Easy going	Shy
Genius prone	Introspective	Patient	Lazy
Well groomed	Self-centered	Leadership	Avoids change
Loyal	Critical	abilities	Self–righteous
Conservative	Guilt ridden	Dry humor	Stingy
Artistic	Indecisive	Conservative	Teases
	Selfish		

A strength when

carried to an extreme

becomes a weakness.

Sanguine

Sam, the Partier

Sanguine Strengths

The Extrovert ——— The Talker ——— The Optimist
Oh, how the world needs sanguines!

These are the **talkative**, wide-eyed, **enthusiastic** people. Their most noticeable characteristic is their **outgoing** nature.

They love to be with people. They are the life of the party. You can usually spot a sanguine in a crowd. They enter with flair and are soon talking with a group gathered around them. They are known as coming into the room mouth first. They are warm, **responsive** people that make friends easily.

One of their shining qualities is that they **live in the present**. They don't worry about the past or have many concerns for the future. They just live each day for that day and enjoy it to the fullest. The bumps in life don't get them down because they dwell in the present instead of worrying about bad past experiences.

Many enjoy having sanguines around because they are **compassionate**. They laugh when people are laughing and cry when others are crying.

One time when visiting my father-in-law in the hospital after he had surgery to remove cancer, I saw a sanguine nurse in action. She walked briskly into the room with a broad smile. She checked the equipment hooked up to him, talked to him, and as she left she turned around and flashed him a big smile. Each time she left his room my father-in-law looked more cheerful because she had been there. My personal evaluation was that she was a sanguine. The clincher came when she had to come back looking for the stethoscope she had left behind. Sanguines are usually **forgetful**.

They are very **friendly**, touching people. It is very difficult for them to talk to others without touching them.

They are more **carefree** than the other temperaments. Their optimism has to do with this but their ability to forget is helpful. While others fret and hold grudges, sanguines tend to forgive and forget.

Sanguine Weaknesses

Samantha wastes time talking.

Sanguine Weaknesses

By now you are probably wondering why it wouldn't be good for everyone to be a sanguine. Let's take a few minutes to look into a few of the weaknesses of this temperament.

It is important to know that what is a strength can become a weakness when it is carried to extreme such as a Sanguine's **compulsive talking**. They can be very entertaining, but when carried to extreme they monopolize a conversation. They also waste much of their time talking on the telephone and/or using a computer.

They can take a simple story and turn it into a sidesplitting one. To make it more interesting they may have to **exaggerate**, to the point of lying to make the story more interesting. They also **talk loudly** to make sure they are heard.

They may appear to be **egotistical**. They are happy people that can accept themselves and others. Some of the other temperaments have low self-esteem and therefore can't understand the self-acceptance of a sanguine.

If you tested high in Sanguine, you are probably quite forgetful. They waste a lot of time just trying to remember where they put something. Because they live in the moment, they often **forget** obligations. Although this is a very annoying characteristic, it can be a real plus because while others dwell over wrongs done to them, a sanguine may have no recollection of the problem at all.

One of their strengths is that they make friends easily. It should also be noted that though they make friends easily; they forget them just as easily. One can meet a sanguine and feel as though they have a dear friend for life whereas the sanguine might not even remember the person's name the next time they meet. This might be looked on as being **fickle** when actually it isn't that at all. They are friendly to everyone the meet and can strike up a conversation with almost anyone that will listen.

Because of their love for the new and exciting they are sometimes **unfocused,** going from one interest to another.

Choleric Strengths

Carl enjoys accomplishing.

Choleric Strengths

The Extrovert---The Doer---The Optimist
Oh, how the world needs cholerics.

If you want to get something done, find a choleric. They are the accomplishers of the world. They are **born leaders** with **organizational** abilities that are unsurpassed. They can pull a project together with an inborn ability. Their natural **boldness** helps them put their ideas into reality.

There is almost nothing a choleric cannot do well. They **do not get discouraged** and quit. A little opposition spurs them on. To them, the difficult will be done today; the impossible may take until tomorrow.

It is very easy for them to make **decisions**. They seem to be able to look at a situation and come up with a solution almost immediately.

Cholerics are very **goal-oriented**. Once they get a goal in view it is almost impossible to deter them until the goal is accomplished. They are also good at multi-tasking.

Sanguines would rather play than work whereas Cholerics **prefer to work**. It would be a rare sight to see a Choleric relaxing. If they are, you will find a doctor advised it for their health. Even if they were relaxing in the sun you would probably find they are reading a book, writing letters or texting. Their relaxation is accomplishing something useful.

The story is told of Thomas Edison's wife trying to get him to take time for himself on his birthday. She got him to agree to take the day and to do whatever he most wanted to do. When she awoke on his birthday she was disgusted to find him in his laboratory working on an invention. When she reminded him he was supposed to take the day for himself, he informed her that he would rather work than do anything else.

They have a very **strong will** that makes them accomplishers. They are also **utilitarian**. For example, if they take on a sewing project it will be something useful or needed like clothes or curtains, whereas if other temperaments sew, they might chose a craft project.

Choleric Weaknesses

Carl campaigns on his soapbox.

Choleric Weaknesses

As we have seen, the Choleric temperament dominant strengths are bold. A person's weaknesses correspond with their strengths, so the Choleric's weaknesses will be strong, bold weaknesses.

Their leadership carried to the extreme makes a choleric capable of being **bossy**. They are known by those around them as wanting things done right, their way, and NOW! Cholerics do not consider themselves bossy. They are just trying to help. Certainly, they reason, everyone would like to know how to improve the way they are doing a task.

Their ability to organize gives them the reputation of being **domineering**. They delegate unimportant tasks and end up doing the majority of the work themselves so it will be done the way they want it done.

One of their favorite sayings is, "If you want something done right, do it yourself." Because they are highly capable they tend to become quite **self-sufficient**.

To them, time is wasted unless something is being accomplished. They are what others would consider a **slave driver**. Cholerics have very **strong opinions**. We are all entitled to our opinion but the Cholerics usually don't keep their opinion to themselves whether anyone else wants to hear it or not.

It is difficult for a person of this temperament to see others sitting idle. They are constantly giving people something to do when they see, what they consider, to be wasting time.

Sanguines are known for being loud. Cholerics are also **loud**. However, their loud is different from Sanguines. They speak with an air of command in their voice. When they speak a hush comes over the room.

Because they are **unemotional** they are not in tune with the emotional needs of others. Getting something accomplished is more important to them than being concerned about the feelings of others. They are known as having a "razor blade" for a tongue. Because they are not aware of how their words sound to others, they come across as being inconsiderate.

Melancholy Strengths

Mel is detail conscious and Genius Prone.

Melancholy Strengths
The introvert -----The Thinker -----The gifted
Oh, how the world needs Melancholies!

People scoring high in this introverted temperament are **sensitive, quiet, perfectionists.** They enjoy the fine arts and are the most **prone to be geniuses.**

They have an amazing ability to size things up, especially people. They can spot a phony very shortly after meeting them. This strength is due to their **analytical** ability.

When they make a decision it is not a rash, spur of the moment one. It is well thought out before it is made.

They like everything **alphabetized, lined up,** and **in its place.** For them there is a place for everything and everything is to be in its place.

A friend of mine likes to hang her clothes out on a clothesline to dry. After taking a temperament test and learning she was a melancholy she told me that she didn't think some of it applied to her. She laughed as she told me about the next time she washed clothes. She hung each item up as she came to it in the basket. After an hour she couldn't stand it any longer. She had to go out, take all the clothes off the lines, sort them by socks, towels, and so on, then re-hung each article in order before she could rest.

They are **loyal friends.** They don't make friends easily but once they do, they are lifelong friends. Of all the temperaments they are the most **artistically gifted.** Many of the great artists, musicians and craftsmen are of this temperament. The world has been given a lot of pleasure because of melancholies. Other temperaments can learn to paint, write or play a musical instrument but you can usually tell when it is the work of a melancholy because there is more feeling of depth to whatever they do.

Melancholies are often misjudged as being **unfriendly.** They simply find it difficult to express their thoughts even though they have strong feelings.

A Melancholy person is very **conservative** and **thrifty.** They can get more for their dollar because they are the coupon clippers and watch for sales people.

Melancholy Weaknesses

Mel relives the past over and over.

Melancholy Weaknesses

While others have been reading the strengths of their temperament, the Melancholies have probably been reading their weaknesses. This is one of their weaknesses; they have a **pessimistic** outlook on life.

Unlike the Sanguine and Cholerics who are extroverts and enjoy being around people, Melancholies enjoy being alone. They prefer to be in a familiar environment because they feel more safe and secure. Because of this they may be looked at as being **unsociable**.

Next on their characteristics is, **rigid standards**. It is their strength of being a perfectionist that, when carried to extreme, turns into this weakness. It is helpful if others understand that they set higher standards for themselves than they do for others.

You can tell what kind of a mood they are in. It is almost as though they have their own personal rain cloud that goes with them wherever they are. Depression is common to them.

There is no other temperament with such abilities, nor any other temperament that feels so inadequate. They interpret casual words or events very personally. This **self-centeredness** causes them inner turmoil stress over trivial matters.

Being **critical** is one weakness they can control. The fact that they are more critical of themselves than of others is also true. If you have children of this temperament, they feel they are a failure unless they get 100's all the time and get the highest grades in school.

If you scored highest in this area, a weakness to watch out for is feelings of **guilt**. They are so concerned about the mistakes they made yesterday and the mistakes they may make tomorrow that they cannot enjoy today.

Indecisiveness is one of their characteristics because they have to weigh <u>all</u> the facts before making a decision.

Phlegmatic Strengths

Phil, the watcher

Phlegmatic Strengths
The Introvert ---- The Watcher ---- The Comforter
Oh, how the world needs Phlegmatics!

These are the all-purpose people. While the Sanguine is talking, the Choleric is planning another project and the Melancholy is considering all the possibilities, the Phlegmatic is sitting **quietly** watching the rest of them and is completely unaffected.

They are **quiet, relaxed** and **easy going** almost all of the time. It takes a long, long time to get a person of this temperament upset.

Being **patient** and **well balanced** they bring calmness to those around them. They never hurry. You can usually tell Phlegmatics by their **slow** mannerisms when they talk, eat, and even walk. They roll along quite well with the good and bad in life, rarely getting upset. When they do get upset they will internalize rather than share their concerns.

Though it doesn't seem apparent at first, they are very good in **leadership** positions. They are not dynamic like the Choleric, but in their quiet way they get things done without upsetting others.

They are **good listeners**. They do not interrupt while someone is talking.

A person with this temperament is usually very **witty**. Their humor is not like the story telling Sanguine. It is a **dry humor** that is spoken at just the right time. When you least expect it they will come out with some simple, quiet statement that is hilarious.

They are **dependable,** which is a good characteristic for anyone.

A phlegmatic is **ultra conservative**. They will not part with a cent if it is not necessary.

Their nature is so peaceful that they will do almost anything to avoid conflict. They do not like to argue.

Phlegmatic Weaknesses

Phil pours cold water on other's ideas.

Phlegmatic Weaknesses

These people sound so perfect you must be wondering if they have any weaknesses at all. But just as their strengths are low key so are their weaknesses

Because they are of a quiet nature and are content be alone, they are considered to be **unenthusiastic**. This is not a problem in their opinion. After all, they feel, why get all worked up about things anyway. They do not seem to care that most of us like a little affirmation occasionally.

Their **stubborn will of iron** makes it nearly impossible to budge them from what they have set their mind to.

Because of their **shyness**, they would rather be in the background. This makes them **spectators** rather than participators.

People testing highest in this area are not highly self-motivated. Others look upon this as being lazy.

One of their quiet weaknesses is having a **self-righteous attitude**. They sit back and watch others and think. "I am glad I am not like the giddy Sanguine, the bossy Choleric or the depressed Melancholy." This attitude is often expressed as **sarcasm** and **teasing**. This characteristic is known as pouring cold water on other people's ideas.

The old adage, "A fool and his money are soon parted" doesn't fit a Phlegmatic. They are very **conservative** and could perhaps give even Melancholies a few tips on how to save a few cents.

Their indecisiveness can be very annoying. They seem to have made a decision to never make a decision, which can be very aggravating to others.

EVERY TEMPERAMENT IS

Oh, how we need the Sanguine!

To give the lift of joy in time of trouble,
For the touch of innocence in a jaded era,
For the wit when we are weighted down,
The lift of humor when we are heavy hearted,
The ray of hope to blow away black clouds,
For enthusiasm and energy to start over,
The creativity and charm to color a drab day.

Oh, how we need the Melancholy!

For the depth to see into the heart and soul of life,
The artistic nature to appreciate the beauty of the world,
The talent to create a masterpiece where nothing existed before,
The ability to analyze and arrive at the proper solution,
The eye for detail while others do shoddy work,
The aim to finish what they start,
The pledge, "If it's worth doing, it's worth doing Right."
The desire to "Do all things decently and in order."

IMPORTANT AND NEEDED!

Oh, how we need the Choleric!

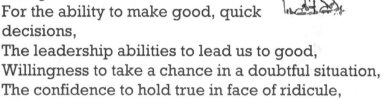

For firm control when others are
losing theirs,
For the ability to make good, quick
decisions,
The leadership abilities to lead us to good,
Willingness to take a chance in a doubtful situation,
The confidence to hold true in face of ridicule,
The independence to stand alone and be counted,
The road map to life when we've gone astray.

Oh, how we need the Phlegmatic!

For stability to stay straight on course,
For patience to put up with provokers,
The ability to listen while others talk,
The gift of mediation, uniting opposite forces,
The purpose of peace at almost any price,
The compassion to comfort those hurting,
The determination to keep their head, while others are losing
theirs,
The will to live in such a way that even your enemies
can't find anything bad to say about you.

Author Unknown

Section II

Next, we will look at comparisons to other theories combined with the Temperament Theory in everyday life.

➤ Temperaments Compared to A B Personalities

➤ Uniquely You (Temperament Blends)

➤ Uses & Abuses

➤ Needs of the Temperaments

Temperament Theory
compared to
Type A, B, and AB Personalities

The **Type A and Type B Personality Theory*** is a personality type theory that describes a pattern of behaviors that were once considered to be a risk factor for coronary heart disease. Since its inception in the 1950's it has become a common way to describe people.

Notice how the description of the Type A parallels the Cholerics and Melancholies,) whereas the Type B is similar to Sanguines and Phlegmatics.

Type A individuals can be described as:
* Impatient
* Excessively time-conscious
* Insecure about their status
* Highly competitive
* Hostile and aggressive
* Incapable of relaxation
* They are often high achieving workaholics who multi-task, drive themselves with deadlines, and are unhappy about the smallest of delays. Because of these characteristics, Type A individuals are often described as "stress junkies."

Type B individuals, in contrast, are described as:
* Patient
* Relaxed
* Easy-going

There is also a **Type AB** mixed profile for people who cannot be clearly categorized. The Type AB appears to be a blend of two or more opposite temperaments, Sanguine/Melancholy or Choleric/Phlegmatic making them more difficult to identify.

*(2)Type A personality behavior was first described as a potential risk factor for heart disease in the 1950s by cardiologists Meyer Friedman and R. H. Rosenman.

Uniquely You
(Temperament Blends)

No one is just one temperament. Everyone has his or her own unique blend. You may have tested out somewhat the same as someone else in the four quadrants, but the number scores will vary. Usually a person is stronger in two quadrants of the temperament square than in the other two. Some people test out strong in three quadrants. When a person tests somewhat similar in all four quadrants, they will have difficulty determining their strengeths and weaknesses.

The **Sanguine/Choleric combination** is outgoing and usually loud. It makes a difference depending on which temperament has the highest score. For example, if the sanguine is the predominant temperament, the person will be enjoy fun and partying. If the Choleric score is higher, person, that person will be more work oriented and serious.

The **Melancholy/Phlegmatic** people are the quiet ones. Both temperaments are introverts; therefore they would rather be in the background than up front. Introverts, unlike the extroverts, are more focused on themselves rather than outside themselves.

Complementary Blends occur when a person's highest score is in opposite quadrants, one an extrovert and the other an introvert. The two temperaments balance each other. The complementary blends are the Choleric/Melancholy and Sanguine/ phlegmatic.

The **Choleric/melancholy temperament blend** produces an extremely capable person. They have the Choleric leadership and drive; but are rounded out by the Melancholy analytical, detail conscious, schedule-oriented mind. These people can accomplish almost anything they decide to do.

The other complementary blend is **Sanguine/Phlegmatic**. The Sanguine makes them warm, friendly, personable individuals and the Phlegmatic tempers the ups and downs that a Sanguine experiences. This blend, especially if the Phlegmatic score is highest, is the easiest of all people to deal with because they are friendly and unassuming.

Opposite Blends occur less frequently. They score highest in two temperaments to the left and right of the square, the **Sanguine/Melancholy** (emotional) and **Choleric/Phlegmatic** (unemotional). These blends are almost dual personalities. For instance, the Sanguine/Melancholy would produce a person that has the Sanguine characteristics of fun and games; as well as the Melancholy part of them that is much more conservative. This combination is difficult because they experience a deep sense of remorse if they let loose and party. Afterwards they go into a deep depression because of their actions. Their emotions run very high and very low.

The **Choleric/Phlegmatic** temperaments are people who do not have the same stresses as the Sanguine/ Melancholy because both of their strongest temperaments are unemotional. They display more of a work-or-not-to-work syndrome. The Choleric's preference is to work while the Phlegmatic's preference is to relax.

Temperament may explain
Behavior, but never
excuses it!

Uses and Abuses of the Temperament Theory

Uses

Self-acceptance — You now have a keener knowledge of yourself by understanding your inherited strengths and weaknesses. You are truly one of a kind.

Self-improvement — By understanding ourselves better we can strive to minimize our weaknesses while improving our strengths.

Accepting others — You can now have a better understanding of why others behave the way they do. Each day we have to interact with others. Understanding the four basic temperaments should make it easier to relate to and accept others.

Abuses

Clubbing others — Understanding the temperaments can be used as a psychological club to bludgeon people. This is never appropriate.

As an excuse — As you know, we all have strengths and we all have weaknesses. Knowing our weaknesses does not give any of us an excuse for unseemly behavior. It doesn't give us the right to go through life not becoming more thoughtful and understanding of others. You can now improve your strengths and attempt to eradicate or minimize your weaknesses.

Categorizing others — It is easy to guess what someone else's temperament is. But it is no help to you or others if you always think of them as a temperament type. You could also be wrong in making snap decisions. Use it for self-improvement, but not to give an evaluation of anyone's temperament unless they ask you to.

Needs of the Temperaments

In order for people to get along well with others it is helpful to have a good understanding of some of their own personality traits that, if modified, would help them in their interactions with others. We cannot change others, only we can change ourselves. Here are some suggestions for the various temperaments.

Sanguines may want to become more reliable and dependable. They may have to work on developing a more self-disciplined life. Their ego may be replaced with genuine humility. They should practice listening instead of constantly talking. Another area to be considered is to make sure they are telling the truth instead of embellishing a story.

Cholerics may need to become more sensitive and compassionate to the feelings of other people. They have to guard against having an angry and/or cruel spirit. Just like the sanguine, they need to add practicing listening more and talking less. Even if they are more capable than others, they should let others lead at times.

Melancholies may want to overcome a critical spirit and learn to forget themselves and think of others. Being overly sensitive is something they may be aware of and need to guard against while working on developing a thankful attitude.

Phlegmatics may need work on developing self-motivation and to recognize and deal with fearfulness. It would also be helpful to those around them if they became more enthusiastic about things. Becoming more enthusiastic would be a delight for other people around them.

The following are things to remember about people with the other temperaments.

Sanguines have a fear of disapproval. Reassure them they have your support. They thrive when they know that they have gained your approval and acceptance. They need an overdose of encouragement.

Cholerics do not accept personal criticism well at first. They do bounce back when hurt or offended because, unlike the Sanguine and Melancholy, they are unemotional. Sometimes they require a little time to evaluate an idea or situation.

Melancholies are not on the inside what they appear to be on the outside. They always look as though they stepped out of a fashion catalog but inside they are a bundle of emotions. They may appear to be unfriendly when perhaps it is actually shyness. They require time to become comfortable with a new situation or environment before they are comfortable expressing themselves. They appreciate sincere approval. Criticism may be devastating to them.

Phlegmatics are the easiest to get along with. They will take things in stride longer than the other temperaments. They will only allow you to push them just so far. When that limit is reached they will just tune you out. They do not like to take risks or make quick changes.

None of us enjoy being demeaned. We need to be aware of how what we are saying may come across to the other person. Sometimes when we say something with perfectly good intentions, the other person may not get the message we intended to convey.

One person may throw a rock and the other person might consider it a boulder.

Choleric throws a rock -------- **Melancholy** catches a boulder

Melancholy throws a boulder ---------- **Sanguine** catches a rock

Sample of a rock and bolder:
Rock: "Hi, what have you been up to lately?"
Boulder: "What is this, an interrogation?"

Section III

The Temperaments in daily activities:

➢ **Gift Buying**

➢ **Driving a Car**

➢ **As Consumers**

➢ **Sitting on Committees**

➢ **Personality Conflicts**

Gift Buying

When taking a person's temperament into consideration it is easier to buy gifts that the receiver will appreciate receiving. The following are some suggestions.

Sanguines are the easiest to buy for because they like anything that is wrapped up. **Gift suggestions:** include gift certificates, dinner out, flowers, videos, and clothing. When they go on a vacation, they want to go and do all the fun things.
Favorite colors: bright vivid colors such as red, orange, green, or yellow.

Cholerics prefer practical gifts that are useful and have a purpose. Something that will help them work more efficiently. Remember if you buy them clothing they prefer something comfortable, warm and useful, **Gift Suggestions:** Useful tools or gadgets are always appreciated.

Favorite Colors: warm autumn colors such as gold, brown, burgundy or soft orange.

Melancholies are the beauty lovers of the temperaments. They know just what they want so you might want to ask them if there is anything they would like to have. It is important that you know just what they would like or they will not be happy with the gift.

Gift suggestions: Flowers, a book, perfume, eating out at a nice restaurant, items for their favorite craft, gift certificate to their favorite store, whatever it is wrap it nicely with a bow that is color coordinated.
Favorite Colors: Subdued winter colors such as muted shades of brown, black, grey, wine.

Whereas **Phlegmatics** don't show their emotions, they probably won't show much enthusiasm regarding gifts, though they are pleased to be remembered.

Gift Suggestions: They are pretty low-key about everything but they do like useful items to make their work easier, a favorite tape of soft music, a box of candy, favorite craft item or a book are always appreciated.

Favorite colors: Soft spring colors, green, yellow, pink or blue.

*Most people appreciate a gift certificate
to a favorite store or restaurant
of their choice!*

Driving a Car

SANGUINES are the drivers that make everyone around them nervous. They drive down the road looking at the person beside them or behind them. They get so involved in talking or listening to the radio that they may tailgate the car ahead of them. Speeding is normal to them; not just on the straight highway but also on curves. At night they get so busy talking they often keep their headlights on high beam when following other cars. They dart in and out of traffic at a high rate of speed.

If you know where they are going, it might be good to remind them when to make a necessary turn before you get to it; otherwise, you may miss the turn or make it on two wheels.

If going on a long trip it would not hurt to take a map with you because they will probably forget to bring one themselves.

Their car is new, shiny and has all possible bells and whistles available. Price was not too much of a concern to them as long as it is what they wanted.

CHOLERIC drivers are easy to spot. They are aggressive drivers that yell at other drivers for not driving properly...their way. Honking the horn, shaking their fist out of the window and swearing at other drivers are some of their identifying characteristics.

When a traffic light turns yellow, to a Choleric, it is a signal to step on the gas pedal before it turns red. If it does turn red a choleric may consider it pink and not take the light seriously.

Their choice of a vehicle is one with practical useful features and is utilitarian, such as a van.

MELANCHOLY people are cautious drivers. Their trips are well planned ahead of time. The rest of the temperaments could learn how to save time and frustration from the Melancholy. Before they leave home they know exactly where they are going and the best route to take. They plan their trips to have all of their shopping done without having to cross the traffic. Before they leave home they know what stores to go to and which side of the road they on and plan accordingly. They even have a written list to make sure they do not forget anything.

This Melancholy is proud to be driving a car that has been reconditioned to its original beauty. They like extras but not if they cost too much. Whatever they are driving, it will be kept in good condition.

TIP: If you purchase pre-owned cars, a Melancholy is a good one to buy from because the vehicle will have been well taken care of mechanically and otherwise.

PHLEGMATIC drivers are referred to as, "Sunday drivers." Like everything else they do, they drive carefully and slowly. They slow down before they are at the intersection and also take off slowly. They, like the Melancholy, take good care of their car but their reason for doing it is so that it will last longer, saving them money.

Sometimes, when the traffic is building up behind them, they will pull off the road to let those wishing to drive faster pass. Then they slowly pull back in the road and continue on their way.

Here comes a Phlegmatic in a car that was a good bargain, which could well be a used car that has proven it gets good gas mileage and is low maintenance or a new one that would be maintenance free.

As Consumers

Each of the temperament types has their own characteristics when it comes to how they handle money and purchase items. This information is invaluable to people in sales. It is also important for each of us to know that when under stress, and for some shopping is stressful, that we often function in our second temperament rather than our first. This accounts for buying items that you are not happy with and after you get home wonder why you bought them.

The **Sanguines** are impulsive buyers with almost no sales resistance. They love to go shopping and check out everything in every store. It is a good idea for them to take a list and stick to what is on it and to remember to tally the checkbook after each purchase to prevent over spending. Their ego plays a big part in their purchasing. Often if others own something, they want it too.

Choleric consumers shop for useful items. Their clothes will be chosen for comfort not style. If buying appliances or tools, they look for such features as what the item will do, how it works, and do they really need it. They do not usually comparison shop. They find what they are looking for and buy it. They are gadget people and tend to pick up items they may never use. They are loyal to stores they have learned to trust.

People scoring high in the **Melancholy** are the super shoppers. They get a $5 item for fifty cents. A high day for them is a double coupon day. They never forget the coupons at home as a Sanguine is apt to do. They have researched every available source of information regarding the item to be purchased. Every purchase is well thought out for quality, as well as bargain prices. They can tell a phony sales pitch immediately. They are very loyal and will do business with someone they know and trust rather than shopping around.

Phlegmatic people are not concerned with the showy extras that the other temperaments would be willing to pay the extra price for. Just as with everything else they do, their decision to purchase an item has been well thought out before they actually make the purchase. They could give even a Melancholy tips on saving money. They make decisions on what to purchase by what it costs and how long will it last. It is important to them that they do not spend for unnecessary features. They too are loyal patrons of a store as long as the price and value are competitive. They will have checked the prices of all the places an item is sold and make their decision on where to buy it by comparing feature to feature and dollar for dollar.

Sitting on Committees

Sanguine committee members do a lot of talking then often forget to listen or follow through. They are great volunteers but may forget to follow through on their commitments. They always appreciate a reminder.

Cholerics are usually the chairperson or would take over if given a slight chance. They can be very dominating and not pay enough attention to the ideas others present. If they feel strongly about a matter they may disregard the committee's decision and do what they please without the backing of the rest of the committee.

Melancholy committee members sometimes drive the rest of the committee to the point of frustration by their constant questions. They can spend hours discussing every intricate detail of each item on the agenda. Regardless of what is being discussed, they can think of objections and possible future repercussions. They are very helpful because they have an ability to see potential issues that could be a problem later on.

It is also important to understand that a melancholy committee member may take the rejection of a proposal they made as a rejection of them instead of the idea presented.

Phlegmatic committee members are easy to get along with as long as the proposal does not cost money. They are quite apt to pour cold water on new ideas. On the positive note, they follow through on things in a quiet way and get things done while others just talk about getting it done.

Insight into Personality Conflicts

There are usually three main reasons for personality clashes:
1. Either the temperaments of the two people are so different they react entirely opposite.
2. Their temperaments are alike and they are both unwilling to compromise.
3. We see our weaknesses in someone else. This often occurs with parents and their children.

Sanguines are such warm, spontaneous, free spirits that they often clash with the more structured temperaments. It is difficult for a Melancholy to tolerate the lack of preciseness in a Sanguine. Constant criticism wounds the ego of a Sanguine and they often retaliate with their best weapon, their tongue. Cholerics get annoyed by their lack of seriousness. Phlegmatics simply tune them out.

Cholerics walk faster, talk faster, think faster and speak their mind faster, with a tone of authority. They are quick thinkers and are usually right. They give their opinion whether others want to hear it or not. Without realizing it, they tromp around in other people's territory without being aware they are being offensive. Their goal is to accomplish their goal regardless of what it takes.

The perfectionism traits of the **Melancholy** can irritate others. They get weary of the Melancholy's concern over seemingly trivial matters. Yet they appreciate their ability to accomplish multiple tasks quietly and proficiently. They are very much appreciated when it comes to getting things done quickly, accurately and with a flare of perfection.

Although **Phlegmatic** people are the least offensive of the temperaments; due to their lack of enthusiasm and their bent towards sarcasm, they can be annoying. Most people enjoy enthusiasm for their ideas. Phlegmatics use passive sarcasm, which catches people off guard, and it takes awhile to realize what was really meant by what was said.

> **WHEN PEOPLE SEE THINGS DIFFERENTLY IT DOESN'T NECESSARILY MEAN EITHER OF THEM IS WRONG.**

Section IV
Family Relationships

➢ Love Languages

➢ Marriage

➢ Parent/Child

➢ Children's Love Languages

➢ Parenting Styles

Love Languages

Dr. Gary Chapman, author of multiple books on *The Five Love Languages*, writes about the importance of being able to express love to your spouse in a way that your spouse can understand. He calls this type of communicating using the five love languages. A person's temperament impacts their love language and the way they express love.

3) The Five Love Languages, Gary Chapman; New York Times, Gary Chapman, http://www.5lovelanguages.com

1. Words of Affirmation *"I Love you." "You are so special!"*
This is when you say how nice your spouse looks or how great the dinner tasted. These words will also build your mate's self-image and confidence.

2. Quality Time

Some spouses believe that being together; doing things together and focusing in on one another is the best way to show love. If this is your partner's love language, turn off the TV now and then and give one another some undivided attention.

3. Gifts

It is universal in human cultures to give gifts. They do not have to be expensive to send a powerful message of love. Spouses who forget a birthday, or anniversary, or who never give gifts to someone who truly enjoys gift giving, will find themselves with a spouse who feels neglected and unloved.

4. Acts of Service
Discovering how you can best do something for your spouse will require time and creativity. Acts of service such as vacuuming, hanging a bird feeder or planting a garden need to be done with joy in order to be perceived as a gift of love.

5. Physical Touch
Sometimes just stroking your spouse's back, holding hands or a peck on the cheek will fulfill this need.

Determining Your Love Language

According to Dr. Chapman, you can discover your own love language by asking yourself these questions:

1. How do I express love to others?
2. What do I complain about the most?
3. What do I request most often?

Speaking in your spouse's love language probably will not be natural for you. Dr. Chapman says, "We're not talking comfort. We're talking love. Love is something we do for someone else. So often couples love one another but they aren't connecting. They are sincere, but sincerity isn't enough."

The best way to find out what your loved one's love language is by asking which of the above love languages do they relate to the most.

Just as with the four basic temperaments there is not often a person with just one love language. If you know the person's temperament blend, it will help to know what their love languages are. The family of origin and life experiences should also be taken into consideration.

Sanguines' love languages are the easiest to identify because they are the most accepting and enjoy almost everything. All five of the Love Languages would be appreciated by a sanguine.

Cholerics are the accomplishers of the world. They are quite self sufficient and not as emotionally involved as the other temperaments. They appreciate Acts of Service because that is how they show love, by doing things for others.

Melancholies are the most emotionally sensitive of the temperaments. They identify and appreciate: Words of Affirmation, Quality Time, Gifts and Physical Touch. Acts of Service are appreciated as long as their preferences are taken into consideration.

Phlegmatics are the least emotional of the temperaments. They would prefer the simple things of life like Time, Words of Affirmation and Acts of Service.

Dr. Chapman's website is, http://www.5lovelanguages.com offers on-line evaluations.

Marriage

The following quotation is taken from The Volume Library, pg. 529, "The whole progress of marriage, from courtship to old age and death, consists of two contrasting themes, dependence and independence."

Learning to gracefully depend on and support another, is perhaps the first key combination for a happy marriage. At the same time, every person has the need to be independent, to be an individual in his or her own right. At its best, marriage can help its partners be both dependent and independent. The challenge of marriage is to reach the balance that makes life richer and fuller for both partners.

In her book, After Every Wedding Comes the Marriage, Florence Litteaur brings out the fact that fairy tales always end happily. She attributes this to the fact that they always end with the wedding.

(3) After Every Wedding Comes a Marriage, Florence Litteauer.

Marriage defies the law of mathematics. We learned in kindergarten that 1+1 equals 2. Marriage says that 1+1 equals 1, two people with their own individuality combining to make one. The Temperament Theory shows us how the combining of two temperaments balances two people into a well-balanced combination.

Understanding temperaments can be very helpful in the marriage relationship. For instance, the old adage "opposites attract" is true. A Sanguine that is naturally outgoing and friendly will probably be attracted to a Melancholy that is steady, sure, and quiet. A Choleric is attracted to a quiet, relaxed Phlegmatic. The opposite is also true. A quiet, steady Melancholy is attracted to the playful Sanguine. A quiet Phlegmatic who likes to be in the background is usually attracted to a dynamic, bold Choleric who enjoys being the center of attention.

A **Sanguine/Melancholy** combination gives the couple the easy, friendly talkativeness of one; and the steady, serene traits of the other, each balancing the other. Two sanguines married to each other would have little steadiness for a well ordered home. A couple I know, him Melancholy and her a Sanguine, always made sure that visitors saw his side of the closet when giving them a tour their new home. She made sure her side was not exposed to view because it was usually cluttered, whereas his space was very neat and orderly. This is typical of this temperament blend.

The **Choleric/Phlegmatic** couple displays a good combination of a leader and a follower. It would be a difficult and stormy marriage with two Cholerics trying to control everything; neither of them seeing they are being difficult and not willing to concede when necessary.

Studies have shown that two Melancholies or two Phlegmatics have a better chance of a successful marriage than two Sanguines or two Cholerics. Of all the temperaments two Phlegmatics would make a success of their relationship because of their ability to get along with anyone. Two Melancholies would work well because they would understand each other and enjoy everything being categorized, alphabetized, organized, and in its designated place.

Problems often begin in a marriage or any relationship when we stop seeing the strengths of our partner's temperament and begin to dwell on their weaknesses. If we do not guard ourselves from this type of thinking, we can lose sight of their strengths and dwell on their weaknesses.

For instance, a person with a Melancholy temperament who likes things neat and orderly will quite possibly marry a Sanguine. Quickly they realize that the first thing on their mate's mind is not keeping things orderly. It seems to them that all their mate cares about is fun and games.

Foremost, to avoid these situations, the couple has to understand their conflicting temperaments; and learn to work together, from their two extremes, toward a comfortable middle point. The Sanguine may need to take things more seriously while the Melancholy may need to somewhat modify their standards to be workable for their fun loving partner. It is also necessary for the Sanguine partner to understand that neatness and order are important to their Melancholy mate to function well.

Choleric/ Phlegmatic marriages are a natural blend. The choleric is always on the go with projects and plans. The phlegmatic's slow, easy pace balances them. This was part of what attracted them to each other. As the marriage progresses the choleric may become impatient with their partner and consider them lazy. because of their the same time being annoyed because of their lack of enthusiasm in their ideas and projects.

The Choleric partner learns to realize it is their mate's Phlegmatic temperament that makes it possible for them to cope with their endless projects and ideas without becoming unglued. Any of the other temperaments would not be able to handle the incessant drive of Cholerics, as well as a Phlegmatic.

On the other hand, Phlegmatic people are sometimes plagued with emotional problems because of their mate's lack of sensitivity to their needs. Choleric people are not emotional and do not understand the emotional needs of others. Fortunately for them, their Phlegmatic partner is also unemotional compared to the Sanguine and Melancholy. In reality, the Phlegmatic is often quite productive; but they do things in such a quiet, unrushed manner others may not be aware of how much they do accomplish.

As often happens, couples may throw in the towel on a marriage when perhaps they could be happy. It gets a lot more complicated when couples split up and remarry, especially if there are children involved. If there are children involved, it is certainly more complicated during a divorce and second marriage. My husband's wise aunt once told me, "It used to be that parents had a lot of children; now, children have a lot of parents and that certainly complicates things."

The sad part is that the same scenario often takes place again when people remarry because they are attracted to the same type of personality traits as their current mate.

The grass may seem greener and sweeter on the other side of the fence, but it is really the same grass.

Parent/Child

Somewhere in the dictionary between the words "bliss" and frustration is the word "children". Parents need all the help they can get raising children. Understanding the temperaments can be very helpful to them.

The first thing to take into consideration is that children inherit their temperament from their ancestors just as they inherit their bone structure, blood type, sex, skin color, and various mannerisms. These were established before their birth by a combination of genes from both parents. Factors such as the environment, childhood training, sex and age will shape and mold them as they grow.

Currently there is no testing to determine the exact temperament of a child. Despite this, one can almost determine what a child's temperament is by observing the child. As with other inherited traits, such as twins occurring every other generation, a child's temperament is often more similar to their grandparents than their parents.

Sanguine Children

Dreaming of a fun day tomorrow.

A Sanguine child is born smiling and friendly. They wake up each morning wide-eyed and ready for another super day. They are pleasant to live with because they are happy and smile a lot. They are playful and fun. They rarely lack friends because to them nobody is a stranger. Everyone is his/her best friend. This child will stand out in a group of children by being the most talkative.

Children of this temperament have a difficult time being alone because they are people-oriented. They will have bursts of sudden anger immediately followed by an apology. They fully intend to be obedient, but they get distracted from their promises easily. A child of this temperament might show up late, sidetracked by something interesting along the way.

Often because of a short attention span, they will go restlessly from one pastime to another.

Because of their undisciplined nature and short attention span a sanguine child should be taught self-discipline at a young age as possible. They may be the class clown and bask in the limelight to the detriment of getting good grades. While basking in the limelight being a class clown, their grades may suffer.

This carefree, happy-go-lucky temperament will be difficult to recognize if they do not have a secure, loving, stable environment. Their self-security depends on being accepted and loved by others, particularly their parents. When this is lacking, they may become solemn and withdrawn.

Sanguine children are good at conning others. They can talk their way out of many situations. They require guidance teaching them to complete what they start; or they may go through life darting from one thing to another.

A child of this temperament may become very unhappy and depressed if he/she is not allowed to be themselves. If you take their carefree spirit away completely they could be headed for emotional trouble. Generally, they are popular and well accepted by their peers.

Choleric Children

Sleep well because they have been
busy when awake.

A Choleric child is known, thanks to Dr. James Dobson, as the STRONG-WILLED CHILD. They come into the family ready to take over and immediately proceed to do so. They are determined to have what they want, when they want it, how they want it and RIGHT NOW! This temperament is the earliest to recognize. People that have a Choleric child quickly learn that raising children is not as easy as they expected it to be.

This child will be incredibly self-sufficient. It becomes a challenge to them when they are told "no". They are spurred on by being told, "no."

Terms used to describe them include "anger" and "determination." They can drive others away because of their strong temperament.

One of their most dominant strengths is that of being born leaders. From an early age this child needs to have defined areas of responsibility and leadership. They will do well when given responsibilities suitable to their age and abilities.

They thrive on activity. A child of this temperament needs to be surrounded with acceptable activities to keep their active mind and hands busy.

Depression can set in on a child of this strong temperament if he/she is not allowed to be themselves. If suppressed, they may not reach their possible potential. My last child is this temperament and though raising him was often difficult, he has grown into an extraordinarily capable and resourceful adult.

Melancholy Children

Restless sleeper

A Melancholy child is quiet and submissive. A child of this temperament is the most likely of the temperaments to be a good student. They will be a teacher's delight, and are the most likely to have high scores. Though they have great potential they often fall far short of their capabilities because they are usually insecure. They require massive amounts of encouragement as to their value as a person. If they bring home a report card with anything lower than all A's, they feel they have failed miserably. They are the most prone to suicide.

They are shy children. Pressing them to be more outgoing could have a reverse effect. They are secure and happy in their own environment. They do not like new situations or being around people they don't know. They feel more secure if they do not go to new places or situations alone.

These children are usually multi-gifted possessing brilliant minds, creative abilities, and are deep thinkers. However, they can have the deepest depression.

Their happiness and security is determined by their perception of what others think of them. Even though they are very capable, they suffer a delusion of inferiority.

Parents of melancholy children should be aware of their sensitive nature. Even though a melancholy child may be more gifted than others, they will be the last one to recognize it. It is helpful if they have sanguine as their secondary temperament. Criticism will cause them to feel inferior. They require a lot of loving support from those around them.

They have the potential of growing up being negative, gloomy, pessimistic self-pitying individuals so it is important they receive a healthy dose of encouragement and acceptance.

They function best in an environment that is neat and orderly.

Phlegmatic Children

Sleeps peacefully all night.

Raising a Phlegmatic child is very enjoyable. They are usually quiet, compliant, easy-going and calm. A child of this temperament is content just lying in the crib looking at the ceiling or wallpaper.

They may be slower than other children in some ways, like walking and talking. They are not in much of a hurry about anything. They are not as expressive or in much of a hurry about anything. They are the spectators of life.

When parents of a Phlegmatic child observe the problems other parents face with their children, they cannot understand why there is even a problem. They pat themselves on the back and wonder why other parents are not in better control of the situation when their children act out.

On the surface, a phlegmatic child would appear to be the perfect child. They are usually quiet. They enjoy reading, and watching television. Anything that requires little effort is their forte. They do not argue or make demands. As the years go by, a parent may realize that a child of this temperament never made much of a fuss, but usually got his or her own way quietly and persistently.

They are slow in everything they do: eating, talking, walking, potty training, etc. Generally they are unmotivated, which can be construed as laziness. If they are not interested in doing something, they won't argue or make a fuss, they will simply ignore the others. Patience is one of their strengths. They are the procrastinators of life.

Because they are difficult to motivate, a checklist of responsibilities is helpful for both the parent and the Phlegmatic child.

Children's Love Languages

Children respond to love languages, as adults do. Their temperament blend will be an indication of which of the love languages that will be most meaningful to them.

1) **Words of Affirmation**—look for ways to reinforce positive behavior. Children thrive on praise.

2) **Quality Time**—time together without distraction conveys love.

Sanguine Children:
Sports activities, they prefer playing more than watching.
They also enjoy watching as long as they have friends over.
Time with adults that love them. Your time and attention is important to them.

Choleric children:
They enjoy doing projects that requires work accomplishing something as well outdoor activities such as camping, swimming, biking.
They are goal oriented so doing projects or playing games with them helps them feel loved.

Melancholy children:
Feel loved when an adult listens to and spends time with them.
Enjoy craft projects.
Quiet times together.

Phlegmatic children:
Enjoy activities that are relaxing such as jigsaw puzzles, reading, nature walks, kayaking, or fishing and computer games alone or with someone that they enjoy being with.

3) **Receiving Gifts**—A gift is a visible symbol of love. Gifts do not have to be expensive. A gift of your time does not cost money but it is precious to a child. A word of encouragement can be a prized gift.

4.) **Acts of Service**—Doing things you know your child would enjoy makes them feel loved. Helping them with their chores, school projects, or an activity they enjoy.

5.) **Physical Touch**—An affectionate touch such as a hug, a squeeze of the hand, a pat on the head or sitting next to you means a lot to a child.

Birth Order

Studying birth order and intelligence as a function of birth order traces its roots back to 1874, when Sir Francis Galton — an Anthropologist and the founder of the Science of Eugenics — published a paper on heredity and intelligence. Dr. Kevin Leman's book "THE BIRTH ORDER BOOK, Why you are the way you are", are excellent resources for this subject.

(4)The Birth Order Book, Why You Are the Way You Are, Dr. Kevin Leman, Spire Books , 1985; Revell, 1998;2009

The research on the concept of birth order or position in the family is enlightening. Years ago little was known about the effects of birth order and its impact on the child's behavior and intelligence. As with all explanations of behavior, there are many variables that factors in each individual's life.

There are many things that shape us into who we are and grow to become. Family structure, the environment in which we live, health issues, training, belief systems and temperaments influence who and what we are.

The next few pages are a brief study into the Birth Order Theory. It constitutes four classifications of children.

1. First Born, *Eldest*
2. Second Born, *Middle-born*
3. Last Born, *Babies*
4. Only Children, *Similar to First Born or Last Born*

According to Dr. Leman It is important to know that if there is a span of five years or more between the birth of children that the birth order can begin all over in the family. Also, a child of the opposite sex of the first-born may have many of the same characteristics of a first-born, though they are not physically the oldest or first-born in the family.

An overview of the characteristic of:

First Born (Eldest)

- Perfectionist
- Little adults
- Responsible and mature for their age
- High achievers
- Good grades in school
- Loyal to family and values family roots
- Respects authority
- Rigid and legalistic
- Overly conscientious
- Dominating, May become good leaders but (often) unpopular with their peers.
- Achievement oriented rather than people oriented
- Attempts to conquer then carry the world

Advantages	Disadvantages
-They receive more attention.	-Under a lot of pressure.
-They are encouraged to achieve.	-Receive more discipline than siblings.
-They are taken seriously.	-More work expected of them.
-They learn leadership skills.	-Expected to be responsible for siblings.
-They are the pacesetter for	-Often forced into the family profession.
siblings.	-Grow up faster.
	-Over burdened with responsibility.
	-Low self-worth, (because they compare themselves with adults).
	-Bear the brunt of anxious parents' first venture with parenting.
	-Pushed to achieve ahead of schedule.

Vocations:

Firstborns usually go into vocations that are data-based compared to people-based. They are more comfortable with things rather than people. They make excellent leaders because they have been leading the other children for years, giving them experience. For example, it is interesting that presidents of the United States are most likely to be first borns.

Second Born *(Middle-born)*

- Often opposite of the first born
- Charming
- Easy going
- Cheerful
- Gentle
- Placid
- Peer-oriented
- Leaves home the quickest
- Unpredictable
- Adaptive and compromising
- Wears an agreeable mask
- Does not want to make waves

Advantages

-First born is buffer and pacesetter
-More friends
-Learns to negotiate and compromise
-Good social skills
-Less fearful and anxious than First Born
-Better chances of being well adjusted as an adult
-Patterns from the older sibling, unlike the firstborn who patterns after adults.

Disadvantages

-Not as many privileges at the 1st born
-Not as much special treatment
-Squeezed between older and younger siblings
-Fewer pictures in the family album
-"Peace at any price" can make them victims
-Feels cheated by life, believes they are the "have not" while the firstborn is the "have" with more rights.

Vocations:

People born in the middle of the birth order usually prefer working in positions that are people-oriented rather than data-oriented. They often choose helping professions.

They can also be very good in leadership positions because throughout life they have learned to deal with people.

Last Born (*Babies*)

Characteristics of:

- Personable manipulators
- Outgoing charmers
- Family clowns
- Uncomplicated
- Rebellious
- Critical
- Impatient
- Impulsive
- Temperamental
- Crave praise and encouragement
- People-oriented
- Self-centered
- Sloppy
- Willing to take risks
- Prefer to remain dependent

- Prefer to remain dependent
- Spontaneous
- Talkative
- Not self-sufficient
- Most popular of siblings
- Charming and carefree
- Playful and lighthearted
- Immature
- Wants to be taken seriously
- High self- esteem if family affirms and encourages them
- Strives to overtake pacemakers or withdraws

Advantages

-Good social skills
-Knows how to have fun
-Relaxed rules

Disadvantages

-Lives in shadow of older children
-Taught by siblings rather than parents
-Does not like to take responsibility for self
-Becomes dependent on others
-Receive more abuse
-Burned-out parents

Vocations: Last Borns are very suitable for people-oriented vocations. They are also adaptable and could work in data oriented vocations though they would prefer jobs or employment where they would be interacting with people.

Only Children
(Similar to First or Last Born)

Characteristics of:

- Many similar characteristics of firstborns, only intensified.
- Can be like the first or last born
- Get along better with people much older or much younger
- Self-centered because they grow up as the center of attention
- Achievement-oriented
- When an adult they behave like an adult, but feel like a child
- Lonely
- Often prefer to be alone
- Acts like an adult
- Worry about doing things right
- High self-worth
- Wish to please
- Gets along well with authority figures
- Can be either dependent or independent
- Have difficulty forming close relationships
- Harbor unrealistic expectations about relationships
- Not competitive or jealous and has difficulty in understanding these traits in others
- Baffled by the normal give-and-take in families with siblings

Advantages

- Abundance of attention
- Capable of a wide variety of things
- Get along with people much older or younger

Disadvantages

- Difficulty relating to peers
- May expect too much of themselves
- Easily become overcommitted
- Need to learn to share
- No buffers between them and adults

Vocations: Not as limited as others because of their wide span of abilities and social skills.

Personal Experience with Birth Order

As an example, in our family there were three boys and one girl. Each child was born within four years of each other. They were born in this order:

First child, a son
Second child, a son (3 ½ years later)
Third child, a daughter (3 ½ years later)
Forth child, a son (2 years later)

The oldest was a typical *Eldest child*. I could depend on him because he was responsible from birth. He listened and followed our wishes and was respectful of authority.

The second son was typical of a Middle-born child. He was charming, easy going and more influenced by friends than his older brother.

Our daughter, our third child, exhibited characteristics of a first-born. She was responsible, a good student, conscientious, and loyal to the family.

Our youngest son was a typical baby. He was a personal manipulator who was independent and willing to take risks. He was also playful but wanted to be taken seriously.

Birth Order & Temperaments Interaction

Knowing temperaments can explain the inherited characteristics of a personality; but understanding birth order gives us a better understanding of the behaviors of people.

For instance, a choleric may not react as bold and forceful if born last in the family. They were taught from infancy that they were not in charge of things; that position belongs to the older siblings. Once they are out on their own, they will probably surprise the rest of the family. They will develop their inherited temperament; but, in the family, they will always be the baby.

A Phlegmatic child that is the first-born will be in the position of leadership in the family. This child will be more assertive than a last-born phlegmatic who will truly love being the baby of the family and being waited on.

As our children grew I began to notice something interesting. Our first-born son and his sister, our third child, both showed similar characteristics. They were responsible for their own behavior and dependable. Their two other siblings were more playful and carefree.

I found it interesting that their temperaments were not the only reason for their behavior. I grouped them into two groups and thought of them as our two "D's,our first-born and his sister, our third child, and our two "J"s, our second and last child. It was not until I read Kevin Leman's birth order book, "Why You Are the Way You Are" that this made sense to me.

Parenting Styles

Parents generally fit into one of three groups, depending on how they manage their children:

5), Parenting Styles, reproduced from the Department of Education http://pediatrics.about.com/od/infantparentingtips/a/04_pntg_styles.html.

Authoritarian, who are relatively harsh, firm, and controlling. (Cholerics and Melancholies)

Permissive, who are accepting, very lenient and laissez-faire. (Sanguines and Phlegmatics)

Authoritative, who are firm without being harsh, and strict without being stifling.

Children of authoritative parents are consistently more confident, poised, persistent, self-reliant and responsible, with less likelihood of delinquency or psychosomatic problems.

Dr. Harold McCurdy, a Smithsonian researcher, studied the development of genius and concluded that children need:

1. Plenty of time to explore and use their own natural creativity,
2. Very little time with their peers and,
3. Warm responsive parents. Children acquire mature thinking skills—the ability to reason consistently from cause to effect—through the normal one-on-one interaction with parents and other special adults.

Those spending more time with parents than with their peers attain this maturity between the ages of 10 to 12, instead of the average ages of 15 to 20. Before that level of maturity they do not understand nor internalize their family's values and can be easily confused by mixed messages from peers, school, music and television

(6) SKY, Jan 1997 pg. 85McCurdy, Dr. Harold, Horizon 5/6

Section IV
Relationships beyond the family

➤ *Friends*

➤ *Teacher/Student*

➤ *In the Workplace*

Friends

Robert E. Sherwood once said, "The happiest person on earth is the man who saves up every friend he can make." Friendship is one of the most important relationships of human beings. As we study friendships we will see that the temperament of a person greatly impacts the type of friend they will be. Let us take a look at the four basic temperaments to give us a better understanding of this.

We will consider **Sanguines** first because this is the temperament that makes friends the easiest. They naturally love people and enjoy being with them. They laugh when others laugh and cry when others cry. They are the life of the party. One of their shining qualities is that they do not hold grudges. First, they might not even take offense. Second, if they do, they will soon forget all about it. They would be the first to apologize. Although they have all these good qualities we must also realize that a person of this temperament is sometimes considered to be fickle. They may be very friendly today and, because they are very forgetful, may not remember who you are the next time you meet them.

A person that is predominately **Melancholy** is more reserved than the Sanguine or Choleric. It takes them more time to size up a person than the gregarious Sanguine. Unlike the Sanguine, they are happy with a few good friends rather than a lot of casual friends. Once they do become your friend you can count on them through thick-and-thin. A person of this temperament does not like attention drawn to them. They prefer to be in the background rather than up front. Because they are perfectionists, it usually takes them longer to get married. They are looking for the ideal person and they would rather wait than settle for less.

Melancholies are often considered to be unfriendly when they are simply cautious with relationships. They do not express their emotions to anyone that is not a trusted, close friend. What Sanguine or Choleric would easily say takes a long time of contemplating for a Melancholy because they are private people who prefer to keep their thoughts to themselves.

 The **Phlegmatic** is the watcher of life. They are the easiest to get along with of all the temperaments. They have many friends because they do not offend easily and are not usually offensive. They are also very good listeners who have compassion and concern for others. Their dry sense of humor is one of their most appreciated characteristics. They often use low key humor to insult people in a way that isn't apparent at first.

For an example, my husband has a Phlegmatic cousin that told us a joke about his wife. He told us that she was working as a test pilot in a broom factory when he met her. What he was telling us was that she was a witch.

They do not say much so what they do say is generally worth hearing. Their one decision in life is to not make any decisions. They are the all-purpose people of life. The world certainly needs some of them to keep the Choleric toned down, the Sanguine organized and the Melancholy cheered up.

 The **Choleric** person is also interesting as far as friendships are concerned. It is important for others to understand them because they often hurt feelings leaving others devastated by their lack of emotion and sensitivity. They are more interested in doing and accomplishing than interacting with people.

One thing that gets them in trouble with others is that they almost always give advice whether people want it or not. Their ability to look at a situation, size it up and come up with a solution along with their natural boldness annoys many people. The reason is they give their opinion instantaneously coming across as a know-it-all. Very seldom do they apologize.

Friends Square

	Sanguine The Talker (BOLD)		Choleric The Accomplisher (BOLD)

STRENGTHS	WEAKNESSES	STRENGTHS	WEAKNESSES
Friendly	Forgetful	Right but unpopular	Soap box master
Enjoys people	Fickle	Leader	Work-a-holic
Life of party	Center Stage	Usually right	Slave driver
Lives in present	Forgetful	Optimistic	Opinionated
Spontaneous	Wants the spotlight	Organized	Unpopular
Carefree	Loud	Decisive	Sarcastic
Apologizes easily	Egotistical	Goal oriented	Dominating
		Enjoys working	

	Melancholy The Thinker (FEARFUL)		Phlegmatic The Watcher (FEARFUL)

STRENGTHS	WEAKNESSES	STRENGTHS	WEAKNESSES
Cautious	Suspicious	Easy Going	Judgmental
Faithful	Insecure socially	Good listener	Avoids decisions
Listens	Skeptical	Quiet	Sarcastic humor
Problem solver	Withdrawn	Inoffensive	Lacks enthusiasm
Well groomed	Self-centered	Leadership ability	Quiet will of iron
Loyal	Critical	Low key	Self–righteous
Conservative	Holds back affection	Patient	Stubborn
Seeks ideal mate	Overly sensitive	Conservative	Stingy
		Witty	

In the Classroom

Raising children to become responsible, capable adults ready to take their place in society is a big job. The old African proverb, *"It takes a whole village to raise a child"* is still in vogue. Even though we are not related to people, we may make an impact that could affect their lives.

Teachers as well as parents share much of the responsibility of preparing children to become adults. An average ratio of students to teacher is about 25 to 1, which makes it difficult for a teacher to spend a large amount of time with any one student. It is helpful to children if parents take an active part in being supportive of their child and their child's teacher.

My husband and I became more actively involved in our children's formal education than most parents. We decided to home school our children back when home schooling was in its infancy in America. It was not easy because there was not teaching materials available geared for parents to use. Parents had to put together their own curriculum and find suitable books and materials to use.

This book is the result of our home schooling endeavor. One of the courses taught was a course I put together on the Four Basic Temperament Theory to be used as a health class. The high school's Guidance Counselor asked me to present it to the adult evening classes. I also began to present the eight sessions at various organizations. The response has been so positive that I decided to put all of the sessions into a book so people could have all of the information in one place rather than eight individual study guides or having to attend a seminar.

Even though knowing and understanding the temperaments of my children was very helpful, I also studied other theories. I found that The Theory of Multiple Intelligences to be very informative when teaching children or adults. This theory has changed the way children are being taught in many schools. The next few pages will show how this theory takes on more meaning when the temperament theory is also taken into consideration.

Sanguine children have a short attention span making it a challenge to hold their interest. They are people-oriented and often disrupt the class. They prefer a lively environment and are often the class clowns. They liven things up wherever they are. This could disrupt a class but it could also lighten things up by giving others something to laugh about thus alleviating tension. One area that needs to be kept on track is the completion of assignments. They are forgetful and need reminders about upcoming deadlines.

Choleric children are very active and assertive and will take over the classroom if possible. They like to be challenged. They can also be a challenge because of their strong will. Because they are the accomplishers, they learn more easily especially if there is a purpose for what they are studying. They learn best with a hands-on approach with projects and life applications. Because they are self-confident and born leaders, they could be a positive influence in the classroom or negative influence by being the class bully.

Melancholy children are the joy of a teacher's career. They enjoy learning. Books are their dear friends. Just tell them what is expected of them and they can be depended on to complete it. Not only will they complete the assignment, they will do it well. They are quiet, respectful and considerate of others and will do more than is required of them. Once they have a concept they have it stored in their analytical mind forever. It is important to give them an abundance of encouragement and honest praise because they are prone to have low self-esteem. Their self-esteem is dependent on their grades.

Phlegmatic children can also be a joy to teach as long as too much isn't required of them. They are slow to complete their work as they are with everything they do. They are quiet most of the time and are prone to day dream their time away. Their humor is dry and unexpected. They are the children that may quietly say something humorous and cause a disruption. They are introverts and usually get along with others. They can also undermine in a way that isn't as noticeable at first as it would be with a Sanguine or Choleric.

Teachers Temperament Square

	SANGUINE **Makes learning fun**		**CHOLERIC** **Disciplinarian**

STRENGTHS	WEAKNESSES	STRENGTHS	WEAKNESSES
Enjoy teaching	Easily distracted	Disciplinarian	Lacks sympathy
Story telling	Exaggerates	Demanding	Lacks toleration
Creative	Disorganized	Dynamic	Slave driver
Sympathetic	May be too lenient	Organized	Impatient
Friendly	Wastes time	High expectations	Inflexible
Carefree	Loud	Decisive	Demanding
Responsive		Strong will	Overpowering

	MELANCHOLY **Creative**		**PHLEGMATIC** **Lenient**

STRENGTHS	WEAKNESSES	STRENGTHS	WEAKNESSES
Talented	Detail Conscious	Easy going	Unenthusiastic
Perfectionist	Rigid standards	Relaxed	Lenient
Organized	Strict	Capable	Lazy
Analytical	Self-centered	Patient	Spectator
Gifted	Moody	Dry humor	Avoids change
Conservative	Critical	Good leader	Self –righteous
Music/Arts	Easily moved to tears	Dry humor	Teases
		Conservative	

Students Temperament Square

	Sanguine **Sam, the prankster (BOLD)**		**Choleric** **Carl, the achiever (BOLD)**

STRENGTHS	WEAKNESSES	STRENGTHS	WEAKNESSES
Friendly	Fickle	Healthy self image	Bossy
Entertaining	Class Clown	Leader	Intolerant
Spontaneous	Forgetful	Organized	Impatient
Carefree	Loud	High achiever	High expectations
Responsive	Craves attention	Completes work	Unpopular
	Dominates	Does not give up	Does not give up
			Dominating

	Melancholy **Melody, the perfect student (FEARFUL)**		**Phlegmatic** **Phyllis, the day dreamer (FEARFUL)**

STRENGTHS	WEAKNESSES	STRENGTHS	WEAKNESSES
Quiet	Overly sensitive	Easy going	Judgmental
Perfectionist	Rigid standards	Dry Humor	Sarcastic humor
Organized	Judgmental	Capable	Lazy
Honest	Self doubtful	Patient	Stubborn
Wants to please	Prefers routines	Leadership skills	Hard to motivate
Multi-gifted	Insecure	Low key	Self-righteous
Conservative	Easily moved to tears	Compliant	Teases

Previous to 1983 educating children was very different. Reading, writing and arithmetic were emphasized. Schools now offer a wide variety of subjects and multiple teaching styles due to research by Dr. Harold Gardner who introduced the Theory of Multiple Intelligences.

The Theory of Multiple Intelligences

One of the most interesting and helpful topics is that of the multiple intelligences. It particularly helped with our children. It was so helpful that I decided to include it in this book because it is an integral part of understanding yourself and others as well.

The following article is from the internet explains this topic far better than I could.

"**The Theory of Multiple Intelligences** was developed in 1983 by Dr. Howard Gardner, Professor of Education at Harvard University. (8) It suggests that the traditional notion of intelligence, based on I.Q. testing, is far too limited. Instead, Dr. Gardner proposes eight different intelligences to account for a broader range of human potential in children and adults. He added to the original list an eighth intelligence, Spatial in 1997".

These intelligences are: (I added the graphics)

1 **Linguistic intelligence** (word smart)

2 **Logical-mathematical intelligence** (number/reasoning smart)

3 **Musical Rhythmic Intelligence** (music smart)

4 **Bodily-Kinesthetic intelligence** (athletics, performing arts)

5

Spatial intelligence (picture smart)

6

Naturalist intelligence (nature smart)

7

Intrapersonal intelligence (self smart)

8

Interpersonal intelligence (people awareness smart)

9 **Existential Intelligence** (have intuition to understand others and the world around them.)

Dr. Gardner said that our schools and culture focus most of their attention on linguistic and logical-mathematical intelligence. We esteem the highly articulate or logical people of our culture. However, Dr. Gardner says that we should also place equal attention on individuals who show gifts in the other intelligences: the artists, architects, musicians, naturalists, designers, dancers, therapists, entrepreneurs, and others who enrich the world in which we live.

Although it is getting better, unfortunately children may have a less common appreciation for their gifting that is not being addressed at school. It would be impossible for a school system to meet the exact needs of every child. This is where parents can step up to the plate by taking notice of their children's interests and encourage them by showing interest in what interests their child. Parents should be supportive and encourage their children's interests, even if they differ from the mainstream.

The theory of multiple intelligences proposed a major transformation in the how a school system is conducted. It suggests that teachers be trained to present their lessons in a wide variety of ways using music, cooperative learning, art activities, role playing, multimedia, field trips, inner reflection, and much more.

The good news is that the theory of multiple intelligences grabbed the attention of many educators around the country, and many schools are currently using its philosophy to redesign the way it educates children.

The challenge was to get this information out to many more teachers, school administrators, homeschoolers and others who work with children, so that each child has the opportunity to learn in ways harmonious with their unique minds.

The theory of multiple intelligences also has strong implications for adult learning and development. Many adults find themselves in jobs that do not make optimal use of their most highly developed intelligences. For example, the highly bodily-kinesthetic individual who is stuck in a linguistic or logical desk-job when he or she would be much happier in a job where they could move around, such as a recreational leader, a forest ranger, or physical therapist.

The theory of multiple intelligences gives adults a whole new way to look at their lives, examining potentials they left behind in their childhood such as a love for art or drama, but now have the opportunity to develop through courses, hobbies, or other programs of self-development.

The next chart is helpful in understanding the eight areas of intelligence. Keep in mind that we are a blend of temperaments so we will see ourselves in multiple categories. There are no absolute correlations as to what intelligences a person has in relation to their temperament, which is more in relationship to genetics.

Intelligence	Often strong in	Likes to	Learns by
1. Verbal-Linguistic	reading, writing, telling stories, memorizing dates, thinking in words.	read, write, talk, memorize, work at puzzles.	reading, hearing and seeing words, speaking, writing, discussing and debating
2. Math-Logic	math, reasoning, logic, problem-solving, patterns.	solve problems, question, work with numbers, experiment.	working with patterns and relationships, classifying, categorizing, working with the abstract

	Often strong in	Likes to	Learns by
3.Spacial	reading, maps, charts, drawing, mazes, puzzles, imaging things, visualization.	design, draw, build, create, daydream, look at pictures.	working with pictures and colors, visualizing, drawing.
4.Bodily-Kinesthetic	athletics, dancing, acting, crafts, using tools.	move around, touch and talk, body language.	touching moving processing knowledge through bodily sensations.
5.Musical	singing, picking up sounds, remembering melodies, rhythms.	sing, hum, play an instrument, listen to music, compose music.	rhythm, melody, singing, listening to music and melodies.
6. Interpersonal	understanding people, leading out, organizing, communicating, resolving conflicts, selling.	have friends, talk to people, join groups.	sharing, comparing, relating, interviewing, co-operating.
7. Intrapersonal	understanding self, recognizing strengths and weaknesses, setting goals.	work alone, reflect, pursue interests.	working alone, doing self-paced projects, having space, reflecting.
8. Naturalist	understanding nature, making distinctions, identifying flora and fauna.	be involved with nature, make distinctions.	working in nature, exploring things, learning about plants and natural events

Section V

Temperaments in the world of business:

- ➤ The Economic Cycle

- ➤ As Consumers

- ➤ Selling to the Temperaments

- ➤ Employer/Employee

- ➤ Aptitudes

The Economic Cycle

the Melancholy designs a product.

the Choleric manufacturers it,

the Phlegmatic

sells it to the Sanguine.

Selling to the Four Temperaments

When we think about selling, we usually think about products or items that are purchased. The following chart is a tool to give insight to interacting with people as well. For instance, if someone is being stubborn, there is no need to argue. What the other person wants is perhaps a logical explanation. Find out why they are resisting.

This method will work much better and have better results than arguing, which usually results in bad feelings and resentment.

Here are some tips when selling to people taking the four basic temperaments in mind. My husband, a successful real estate broker, found this information helpful when dealing with clients.

CHARACTERISTIC	ACTION TO TAKE
KNOW IT ALL *(Choleric)* *(Sanguine)*	-Reassure them of your expertise. -Shorten presentation.
HESITANT *(Phlegmatic)* *(Melancholy)*	-Do not offer to many choices. -Be definite and firm in voice and manner to gain their trust. -Find out why they are resisting. -Give them time to make a decision.
STUBBORN *(Phlegmatic)* *(Melancholy)*	-Deal with Logic. -Find out why they are resisting. -Appeal to the client's reasoning. -Chart reasons for and against.
COMPLAINER -Negative -Apprehensive -Distrustful *(Melancholy)* *(Choleric)*	-Be well prepared with facts and documentation. -Show facts and benefits on paper. -Avoid arguments.

CHARACTERISTIC	ACTION TO TAKE
TIGHTWAD *(Choleric)* *(Phlegmatic)* *(Melancholy)*	-Stick to your price. -Justify with benefits.
JOKER *(Sanguine)*	-Go along with the joke. -Don't deviate from your presentation. -Tell narrative, fun, interesting stories.
SELF-ABSORBED *(Choleric)*	-Pre-occupied -Put something in their hands. -Get them to make eye contact.

The Temperaments in the Workplace

Many of the courses given in vocational training classes to help students know which careers to pursue are based on the Four Basic Temperament Theory.

Because temperaments are a big part of the work area the temperament theory is a very helpful tool to make good career choices or personnel placement. The following are suggestions.

As the accomplishers in life, Cholerics are goal-oriented and very productive in whatever position they hold. They are good at organizing and visualizing, making it easy for them to get things done with as little effort and time as possible. They also thrive on opposition, it makes them determined to follow through no matter what obstacles come their way.

Carl,
The accomplisher

They enjoy working and can become workaholics. They are excellent in managerial positions though they are known for not having tact and often step on others to get where they want to be on the ladder to success.

Melancholies are excellent in the work area. An employer gets their money's worth with melancholy employees. They are sticklers for details, neat, conscientious and have excellent work ethics. They do not like to leave projects undone. They especially like to work with facts, graphs, charts, numbers, lists or details of any kind. They prefer behind-the-scene positions. They require encouragement. A pat on the back and/or a word of appreciation will be richly rewarded in loyalty. If their secondary temperament is choleric they will prove to be well worth their salary.

Mel, Detail Conscious

Phlegmatics fit well in the workplace. They require a detailed job description to follow. They get along well with others, which promotes any workplace running more smoothly. They do not like controversies and will do all within their power to avoid confrontations. They function better than the other temperaments when under pressure. They persevere despite workplace pressures. If they are not kept busy they will waste time.

Phil,
The quiet
accomplisher

Sanguines excel as speakers, sales people and in public relations. Anything that requires talking and being around people is suited to their temperament. They have good intentions and often volunteer, but are forgetful and may forget to complete what they promised to do. Their strengths are not in a position where details or paper work are important without a temperament blend of any of the other three giving them the stability of a routine.

Sam,
The charmer

In the workplace, people often function in their second-highest scoring quadrant, or possibly the third or fourth depending on the amount of stress involved. When at home, the highest scoring quadrant usually dominates.

The Four Temperaments
In The Workplace

Sanguine
Sam,
The
Talker

Choleric
Carl,
The
Achiever

STRENGTHS	WEAKNESSES	STRENGTHS	WEAKNESSES
Creative thinker	Lacks follow through	Goal oriented	Intolerant
Means well	Clown	Detail conscious	Dominating
Starts flashy	Loud	Visionary	Impatient
Volunteers	Forgetful	Organized	Slave driver
Enthusiastic	Craves attention	Enjoys working	Unpopular
Friendly	Distracts others	Completes work	Controlling
Inspirational	Easily distracted	Doesn't give up	
		Self-sufficient	

Melancholy
Mel,
The
Accurate

Phlegmatic
Phil,
The Slow and
steady

STRENGTHS	WEAKNESSES	STRENGTHS	WEAKNESSES
Super worker	Overly sensitive	Easy Going	Shy
Perfectionist	Rigid standards	Dry Humor	Sarcastic humor
Organized	Insecure	Capable	Lazy
Detailed	Prone to depression	Patient	Stubborn
Analytical	Self-depreciating	Capable leaders	Difficult to motivate
Good solutions	Insecure	Low key	Self –righteous
Multi- talented	Tearful	Compliant	Teases
Dependable			

Section VI

Stress and the Temperaments:

- ➤ Territorial Boundaries

- ➤ Stress Overview

- ➤ Stress, Temperamentally Speaking

- ➤ Anger/Fear

- ➤ Emotional Responses

Territorial Boundaries

Territorial boundaries are a large part of everyday life, even animals understand the concept.

I learned this by observing our little pet Sheltie dog, Jamie. I was concerned because she began acting strangely.

This happened when we lived way out in the country on a dirt road. Our house was set back quite a distance from the road. She had acres to call her own. Yet she started refusing her usual walk to avoid the driveway. Instead, she started taking a short cut from the house and down across the pasture rather than walk down the driveway with us.

Jamie knew something I didn't. My neighbor's dog had staked its claim to our yard right up to the steps leading to our kitchen door.

The neighbor's dog had, in the past, defended her territory by attacking Jamie. Now Jamie was protecting herself by avoiding our neighbor's dog's claim to our driveway.

People also have their own territorial space. Though we don't mark definite physical boundaries as an animal would, we all have areas that we protect. This space may be a physical realm, such as our home or mental realm, blocks of space we will choose to let others into or keep them out. Only we are a little more civil about protecting our territory than an animal would be, yet we still defend our territories in various ways.

The difference in the animal kingdom and that of human beings is that animals know distinctly where the territorial boundaries are, but with people the boundaries are not clearly defined and apparent to others.

The space we claim can depend on the situation. Dr. Edward T. Hall, Professor of Anthropology at Northwestern University, (9) has listed the territorial zones into four distinct zones in which most of us operate. They are:

> Intimate distance – from touching to 6-18 inches.
> Personal distance – 1 ½ feet to 4 feet.
> Social distance – 4 feet to 7 feet.
> Public distance – 12 feet to 25 feet.

We are not comfortable when others come too close. This information is used in many situations. Sigmund Freud, founder of the discipline of psychoanalysis, arranged his sessions so that people would lie on the couch while he sat in a chair out of the patient's sight. By doing this he was making sure he did not intrude on the patient's personal space.

On the other hand, police interrogation of criminals is used as a way to deliberately intrude on the suspect's space. The following is from Body Language by Julius Fast.

"A textbook on criminal interrogation and confessions suggests that the questioner sit close to the suspect and that there be no table or other obstacle between them. Any kind of obstacle, the book warns, gives the person being questioned a certain degree of relief and confidence."

The book also suggests that the questioner, though he may start with his chair two or three feet away, should move closer as the questioning proceeds, so that ultimately one of the subject's knees is just about between the interrogator's knees.

This physical invasion of the suspect's territory by the police officer, the crowding in as he is questioned, has been found in practice to be extremely useful in breaking down the prisoner's resistance. When a man's territorial defenses are weakened or intruded upon, his self-assurance tends to grow weaker."

Intruding in another's territory
We can physically intrude into a person's space in such ways as:
- ✓ getting too close as with the interrogation method used by the police,
- ✓ by touching someone, or even
- ✓ by staring at them.

We can also mentally intrude in a person's space by:
- ✓ talking to them,
- ✓ asking questions they consider too personal,
- ✓ looking at them too long,
- ✓ disagreeing with them,
- ✓ interrupting them while mediating or enjoying alone time,
- ✓ talking about them on the telephone when they can hear,
- ✓ replacing them in a relationship, at work, or in some other way.

We can tromp all around in another person's territory unaware of how we are intruding on them. For a clearer understanding, let's take a look at territorial boundaries in the light of day-to-day living.

Let's start with two people getting married. Each one of them has their own territorial space. Each has a different childhood background, birth order, expectations, and personality. There is a period of adjustment when both of them have to readjust their space. Ideally if all goes well, they are able to redefine their territorial boundaries and eventually the two are one in many ways.

One of my favorite territorial boundaries stories involves my father-in-law and his new wife. He was 75 and she was in her late 60's when they got married. They had been married for about a year when this incident took place.

They were eating out in a restaurant one evening when my mother-in-law became very upset. A former female co-worker of his came into the restaurant. They greeted each other with a quick hug. Then she sat down with them and they chatted a few minutes. My mother-in-law did not express her thoughts to him in the restaurant but waited until they were home. Her territory (him) had been invaded by another woman and she did not like it. It surprised me because I didn't expect a couple their age to have spat over jealousy.

Children are comparatively easy to raise at first but it does not take long for parents to notice that their precious little one have staked out some of their own territorial boundaries. This shows up when another child tries to play with their toys or when mom and dad set limits. This intensifies as the child grows.

It is a relief to both the parents and children when the children become mature enough to handle what they had wanted to make decisions on prematurely.

After this establishing of space is accomplished, when the child is mature, it frees parents and children to be friends with a mutual respect for each other's private space.

Territorial boundaries play a large role in many areas of our lives. Wherever there are people, there will be territorial boundaries.

Organizations can a hotbed of territorial boundary issues. They are made up of a variety of people of all sizes, shapes, colors, and ethnic backgrounds. Members who have strong loyalty to their organization will feel very protective. It helps to take territorial boundaries into consideration when any group of people is involved.

Next, we will review the four basic temperaments to see how territorial they are.

 Sanguines are not really concerned about territorial boundaries. Neither are they troubled if someone is in their space. They also do not have keen discernment to realize that they are in someone else's territory.

 Cholerics are more territorial than the sanguine but can deal with it. Neither the sanguine or choleric mind being in someone else's space, the difference is the Choleric might be there by choice not caring about how the other person feels, whereas the Sanguine is there simply because they are both in the same place.

 **Melancholies** are the most protective of their space because they are very private people.. It is uncomfortable for them to have others around unless it is on their terms. Likewise, they are very intuitive when they are in another's territory. They are much more comfortable in familiar environment than new situations.

 **Phlegmatics** guard their space more than the other three temperaments. They enjoy being alone and enjoy a peaceful, quiet environment. They simply and quietly tune others out.

STRESS Overview

Next we will look into health issues that can be caused when personal territorial boundaries are violated.

Your temperament impacts how you handle stress. People deal with stress with two emotions:

Anger and/or Fear

Although stress is often negative, there are times it can be beneficial. For instance, stress makes us grow. Physical stress on the body causes the bones to grow stronger and the muscles to develop. Stress causes the heart to pump harder and faster, thus strengthening it.

We will be taking a look at harmful stress in this segment. We need to understand something basic about people before we can fully understand how stress affects them.

There is a common denominator regardless of what temperament or blend of temperaments we are. Each of us possesses selfishness as part of our character. Often, conflicting situations would not take place if we were as concerned about others as we are of ourselves.

Let's see how this would manifest itself in the four basic temperaments.

Sanguines are fun loving and happy most of the time; especially if things go the way they want them to. If things are not going the way they want them to, they will usually react with an outburst of verbal unpleasantness.

Cholerics can become very disagreeable when they are not in control. Their selfishness manifests itself in controlling not only situations but people as well.

Melancholies do not often speak out when they are angry. They maneuver people by generating their negative feelings. Psychological warfare is waged on anyone between them and what they perceive should be. Silent or not, it is still coercing others.

Phlegmatics, though peaceful by nature can be pushed just so far. When things do not go as they wish, they can become very upset. They are more apt to be quiet and leave, rather than stay and talk out a problem, or they may decide to undermine rather than deal with their passive anger.

Stress, Temperamentally Speaking

Sanguines

Extrovert/Emotional (Anger)

Sanguines are last-minute people. They do not spend much time planning ahead. This would cause a lot of tension for those of another temperament, but Sanguines do quite well by improvising on the spur of the moment.

Their incessant talking causes them a lot of stress. It is not the talking but rather the aftermath of their talking. For instance, the length of their conversations cuts deeply into time for completing tasks. They use excuses like: "too much to do" or "not enough time" when they simply have talked their time away.

Though their talking may be a problem to them, it is also one of their best assets because they can talk themselves out of most situations. They can charm others and often use this means to handle stressful situations.

Sanguines tend to be screamers. They often talk too loudly. Also, they may not have a firm grasp on all the facts. This may not be an issue with them because they often embellish a simple story to make it more interesting and impressive.

They weep when others weep and laugh when others laugh. They also laugh when under pressure.

Because it is difficult for them to face unpleasant situations squarely, they are more prone than the other temperaments to lie or tell unrelated stories to relieve a stressful situation.

Their ability to forgive and forget helps them to prevent unpleasant situations from destroying their happiness.

CHOLERICS
Extrovert/Unemotional (Anger)

Cholerics tend to create more stress than the other temperaments. They thrive on it until the body breaks down with physical problems, such as high blood pressure, ulcers or possibly a heart attack.

They often over commit themselves because they see so much to be done and want to do their part. A strong Choleric would rather do everything because they feel no one else can do it right. They are the quality controllers of the universe. If they would delegate responsibilities they would be less busy. They cannot stand to see something not being done right, (their way) without trying to straighten it out. They may give their opinion even if isn't wanted. Surely, they think, others would appreciate knowing how to do it right.

They thrive on opposition. When others would fold up and quit, the Cholerics are spurred on. They do not wallow in self-pity over an insult, failure, or rejection. They simply get started on another project. Remember, with them the difficult will be completed today—the impossible may take until tomorrow.

Cholerics sometimes do not care whether their methods are legal, honest, or fair as long as they accomplish their goal.

When under pressure they become impatient which makes them critical and demanding. Because they are not emotional, they are often cruel and unkind. They may become very sarcastic when provoked.

As employers, they often experience a high turnover rate in their employees.

In a family setting, their families learn to give them a lot of room. Cholerics control their families with an iron hand and no one wants to be responsible for a sudden burst of anger from them. Their principle weapon is their razor blade tongue.

It is important for Cholerics to set their priorities in order. Many of them spend their life accomplishing, at the expense of their own health and family.

Melancholies

Introvert/Emotional
(Fear)

Because of their perfectionist ways, everything is intensified with a Melancholy, especially in the area of stress. They rule their family with their moods, so no one wants to say or do anything for fear of sending them into a state of depression.

Much of the stress they deal with may not even be necessary or well founded. Their energies are spent worrying about things that may not be worth their mental energy or time. One Melancholy described his life as, "I cannot enjoy today. I spend my time worrying about the mistakes I made yesterday and the ones I might make tomorrow that I cannot enjoy today." The other temperaments attitude is more like, there is nothing we can do about yesterday, it is gone; and tomorrow may never come for us, so why waste time worrying about it?

They internalize pressure to be what they think others are expecting of them. The more they internalize the more they get themselves worked up and sometimes break under the self-induced strain. This can manifest itself with bizarre behavior, driving them to acts of violence.

Melancholy/Cholerics are the epitome of workaholics. They gain their acceptance by doing their work well and react to stress by intensifying their efforts.

They can turn a relaxing walk into a pressured-filled activity.

Phlegmatics
Introvert/Unemotional
(Fear)

Of the four basic temperaments, Phlegmatics cope the best with emotional stress; in fact, they tend to ignore it even exists. Avoidance is their favored reaction.

Because their one great decision in life is to never make a decision, they become gifted procrastinators. If you try to push them, they dig in their heels and resist all the more. They have the ability to ignore what is going on around them.

If it is possible, they will leave unpleasant tasks, such as disciplining their children or discussing a problem with a neighbor, to others rather than deal with it themselves.

Because they detest controversies, they will avoid them if at all possible. They will tolerate something for a long time without letting you know they are unhappy.

Instead of getting into an argument they will put up with being treated badly just to keep peace. This 'peace-at-any-price' attitude makes it difficult when someone else is trying to work out an issue with them. They may even leave a relationship rather than letting the other person know there is a problem.

At times they will blame others for their mistakes because they do not like to face responsibility for their own behavior. "That's my story and I'm sticking to it." is one of their favorite statements.

A phlegmatic will often daydream to escape reality.

ANGER

Choleric and Melancholy Temperaments

Anger is one of the two major causes of stifling communication. Anger is more a matter of a person's temperament than their gender.

ANGER MANIFESTED AS:
Bitterness
Malice
Envy
Resentment
Intolerance
Criticism
Revenge
Sarcasm
Hatred
Violence
Jealousy

RESULTS OF:
Relationships destroyed.
Children subjected to emotional tension that staggers the mind.
Emotionally scarred people everywhere.
Physical abuse.

HEALTH COMPROMISED:
High blood pressure,
Heart attacks,
Colitis,
Arthritis,
Kidney stones,
Gallbladder problems,
Bleeding ulcers.

With a child we call it an outburst of anger a "tantrum"
With an adult, we call it "nerves."

Fear

Sanguine and Phlegmatic Temperaments
(Suppressed Anger)

FEAR IS MANIFESTED AS:

Worry
Doubt
Anxiety
Suspicious
Feeling of inferiority
Timidity
Indecisiveness
Depression
Withdrawal
Loneliness

RESULTS OF:

Paralyzes emotion, which inhibits or restricts normal feelings of love, confidence and well-being.

Triggers a negative thought pattern which breeds other emotions a person already has. It can gain momentum like a giant snowball and consume a person's entire life.

Fear is to your emotions what cancer is to the body; it invades the total person.
Mental and emotional collapse.

HEALTH IS
COMPROMISED:

Headaches
Ulcers of the stomach and intestines
Kidney disease
Heart trouble
Stroke
Gallbladder problems
Colitis
High blood pressure
Arthritis
Impotence in men, Frigidity in women.

Emotional Responses of the Temperaments

Sanguines are very emotional. Everything with them is wonderful or dreadful. There seems to be no middle ground with them. They are either emotionally high or low, usually high because they tend look at the bright side of things.

Cholerics do not have the extreme emotional ups and downs of a Sanguine because they are not concerned about others; they just want to get things done their way and NOW!

Melancholies, like the Sanguines, have highs and lows but their highs are lower and their lows are higher for a longer periods of time.

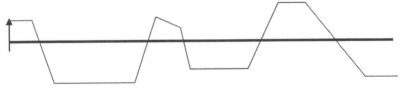

Phlegmatics are easy going and adaptable people who want above almost anything else to avoid confrontation. When they do get upset it may not even be noticed.

Section VII

Spiritual Temperaments
(Gifting)

➤ Overview

➤ Love is a Fundamental Human Need

➤ Everyone is Gifted

➤ Biblical Examples

➤ Jesus as our Example

➤ Spiritual Gifting

"And let us consider how we may spur one another on toward love and good deeds."
Hebrews 10-11 NIV

Overview

A person's faith system has a huge impact on their interactions with others. The Four Basic Temperament Theory is a tool that can be used to identify the gifting promised in the scriptures. These gifts are to encourage and strengthen each other.

There are many verses throughout the bible that give us information about the gifting of individuals as in I Corinthians, chapters 12 & 13.

"There are different kinds of gifts, but the same Spirit. There are different kinds of service, but the same Lord. There are different kinds of working, but the same God works all of them in all men.". Corinthians. 12:4-6.

Wisdom	*Discernment*
Knowledge	*Multilingual*
Faith	*Interpretation of languages*
Gifts of healing	*Helping others*
Miraculous powers	*Administration*
Prophecy	*Love*

In this section we will take a look at the four basic temperaments with the spiritual gifting mentioned in the Bible. By doing this, one can more easily discern where their gifting is the strongest. Two things to take into consideration regarding gifting:

1. It is important that the 2nd, 3rd and 4th temperaments be taken into consideration as well as the 1^{stt}.
2. The spiritual growth of an individual

"The Lord is disappointed when His people place a low estimate upon themselves. He desires His chosen heritage to value themselves according to the price He has placed upon them. God wanted them; else He would not have sent His Son on such an expensive errand to redeem them."

10) Desire of Ages, E.G.White, www.white estate.org/books/da/da73.html, pg. 668,(10).

Everyone is Gifted

We are all born with abilities (gifts), some more noticeable than others. If you think you not have any gifts, let me tell you a story I read about a young man named Brian.

Brian lived in a group home. Brian was different from the others inasmuch as he was totally dependent on the others. He could not live without them. They took care of his every need. One evening there was a special event going on in the community that everyone wanted to attend. The person who wrote the story told of how disappointing it was for her to have to stay home because it was her turn to take care of Brian.

When she was alone with Brian, she began to think about having to stay home while the others were enjoying the evening's activity. The more she thought about it, she realized that Brian was a blessing, not a burden. He was the unifying element to the rest of those living in the house. The gift he gave everyone else in the house was that of being needed. He gave all of them a purpose for life, taking care of him. He turned the house into a home full of people who cared about each other.

If Brian did all that for others while he himself was helpless, think of what your gifts are that could be a blessing to those around you.

Everyone is born with natural gifts, which we think of as abilities. They are part of who we are. The world teaches us to use these gifts to be all that we can be.

For a Christian there is more meaning to life than just serving oneself. The gifts are given to them to use for the benefit of others and to show them what their heavenly Father is like.

An understanding the Four Basic Temperaments give us insight into the creativity of our creator. None of us are exactly the same as someone else. Even identical twins have a few characteristics that differ from their sibling. We are to appreciate who we are as individuals and to be respectful of others as well.

Biblical Examples

**Peter,
The Impetuous**

Peter displays the characteristics of a **Sanguine.** He is referred to as, "Impetuous Peter" because he would speak and act before he thought things through, such as walking on water. When he saw he was standing on water he became fearful and began to doubt. At the trial of Jesus he denied knowing Him. Yet he was the one who chose to be crucified upside down because he felt unworthy to be crucified as Jesus had been.

**Paul,
Prolific
Writer**

Paul is a good example of a **Choleric.** It is easy to tell his temperament because he had to be stricken with blindness before he would listen to God speaking to him. Before his conversion he was a Pharisee known for his zeal in persecuting the early Christians. It took being struck with blindness to get his attention. He wrote 14 of the 27 books in the New Testament. He is attributed to being one of the founders of the early Christian church.

**Moses,
The Trusted**

Moses chose to lead God's complaining, grumbling people out of Egyptian bondage over being the king of Egypt. God entrusted him with the original Ten Commandments God wrote on stone. His leadership and perseverance to always do what is right indicates a strong **Melancholy** temperament.

**Abraham,
Faith**

The gentle, peacemaker Abraham is a living example of a **Phlegmatic.** God told him to move to a foreign country. He complied leaving his family behind and became the father of the Hebrew nation. Abraham exhibited the negative characteristic of being fearful and untruthful when he was fearful of losing his life, but he repented and became an example of being someone of faith with human frailties just like us.

Spiritual Temperaments
Examples from the Bible

	Sanguine Peter Impetuous		Choleric Paul Prolific Writer
STRENGTHS	**WEAKNESSES**	**STRENGTHS**	**WEAKNESSES**
Bold	Impetuous	Born Leader	Controlling
Friendly	Unstable	Bold	Overpowering
Enthusiastic	Forgetful	Organized	Opinionated
Optimistic	Loud	Decisive	Self-sufficient
Compassionate	Egotistical	Goal Oriented	Intolerant
Responsive	Betrayer	Enjoys Working	Work-a-holic
	Melancholy Moses The Trusted		Phlegmatic Abraham The Follower
STRENGTHS	**WEAKNESSES**	**STRENGTHS**	**WEAKNESSES**
Perfectionist	Reserved	Patient	Untruthful
Analytical	Fearful	Quiet Leader	Fearful
Quiet	Distrusts self	Dependable	Distrustful
Gifted	Low self-	Relaxed	
Sensitive	confidence	Trusting	
		Loyal	

As I studied the temperament theory I found it very interesting that Jesus exhibited characteristics of all four of the temperaments during His earthly ministry.

Sanguine, He mingled among the people teaching and healing.

Choleric, He drove the money changers from the temple because they were using the temple as a market place.

Melancholy, He treated people with respect and kindness.

Phlegmatic, He was kind and thoughtful.

Jesus, Temperament Square

He exhibited all the strengths and none of the weakness of each temperament.

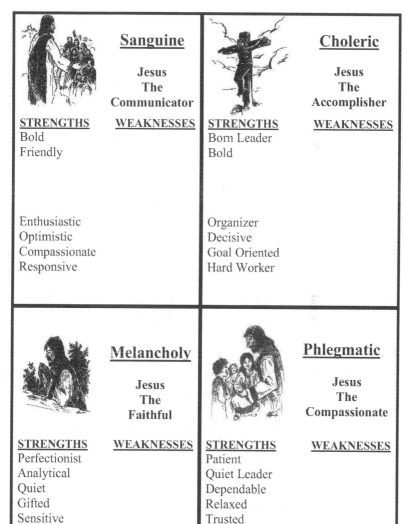

Sanguine

**Jesus
The
Communicator**

STRENGTHS   **WEAKNESSES**
Bold
Friendly

Enthusiastic
Optimistic
Compassionate
Responsive

Choleric

**Jesus
The
Accomplisher**

STRENGTHS   **WEAKNESSES**
Born Leader
Bold

Organizer
Decisive
Goal Oriented
Hard Worker

Melancholy

**Jesus
The
Faithful**

STRENGTHS   **WEAKNESSES**
Perfectionist
Analytical
Quiet
Gifted
Sensitive
Loyal

Phlegmatic

**Jesus
The
Compassionate**

STRENGTHS   **WEAKNESSES**
Patient
Quiet Leader
Dependable
Relaxed
Trusted
Loyal

Gifting / Talents

Sanguine

The Communicator (BOLD)

STRENGTHS	WEAKNESSES
Helping	Disorganized
Loving	Forgetful
Enthusiastic	Talks to much
Optimistic	Self-centered
Compassionate	
Responsive	

Choleric

The Accomplisher (BOLD)

STRENGTHS	WEAKNESSE
Wisdom	Stubborn
Knowledge	Takes over
Discernment	Opinionated
Multilingual	Inconsiderate
Administration	

Melancholy

The Caring FEARFUL

STRENGTHS	WEAKNESSES
Wisdom	Fearful
Faith	Introspective
Discernment	Negative
Loving	Moody
Wisdom	Self-centered
Helping	High standards

Phlegmatic

The Server FEARFUL

STRENGTHS	WEAKNESSES
Administration	Doubts
Healing	Selfish
Wisdom	Judgmental
Languages	Unmotivated
Discernment	Avoids change
Loyal	Limits God by Unbelief

Section VIII

A-NEW-START
(Acronym for Physical Health)

A ttitude

N utrition
E xercise
W ater

S unshine
T emperance
A ir
R est
T rust in Divine
power

So far we have looked at how our temperament impacts our emotions. In the next few pages will focus on physical health taking what we have learned about our temperament into consideration.

These principles have been available for many years, but it was not until several years ago when I experienced a heart attack and began experiencing other issues that I took them seriously.

A NEW START is an acronym for a complete physical health makeover.

First, let me tell you about Mr. Walker.

He lived in a town next to where I live. He had serious heart problems and was hardly able to walk. His wife had read about a place called Weimar Institute, a health reconditioning center in California that was doing remarkable things for people like her husband. They used the A **NEW START life-style changing program.** She made arrangements for them to go there.

His doctor told them that he probably would not survive the trip. His condition was so severe that he had to be pushed up the ramp in a wheelchair to get into the plane.

In a few weeks they returned home. He was not wheeled off the plane in a wheel chair, he walked off the plane. Not only did he walk off the plane, he walked five miles every day for exercise. He also split and carried in the firewood for his wood stove. His quality of life was so improved it was the talk of the town.

After I experienced a heart attack I decided to put the simple principles of A NEW START into practice. It worked for me too. The good news is that these simple health principles have helped people for many generations and are still available free of charge.

Statistics are showing that as a nation we are in trouble healthwise, physically and emotionally. What used to be health issues of the older generation are now showing up in young children.

For instance, heart problems formerly considered a disease of the elderly, are showing up in young children because of poor diet and inactivity. The crisis is not only impacting our health and quality of life; it is also costing far more than it should for our nation's health care programs, resulting in a larger tax burden for taxpayers.

The next few pages will give some history of a time when the simple health principles put forth in this chapter were used with great success in improving the quality of life for people who applied the information to themselves. They worked then and still work now.

The name Kellogg is very familiar to everyone. When we hear it, breakfast cereals come to mind. Dr. John Harvey Kellogg (1852-1943) was a doctor and administrator of the Battle Creek Sanitarium in Battle Creek Michigan. The Sanitarium was the most famous health institution in America from its beginning in the 1880's until World War II. They made Battle Creek the breakfast cereal center of the world.

(11) Willard Library, 7 West Van Buren Street, Battle Creek, MI 49017 —— 269.968.8166, *(pg.101).*

Dr. Kellogg put Battle Creek Sanitarium on the map as the place to recuperate and rejuvenate. With over 400,000 guests and a staff of 1,800 the Sanitarium became a destination for both prominent and middle-class American citizens. It was nicknamed "The San" by its clients and was a popular place for the rich to go for a health retreat and dieting.

He was a brilliant surgeon who introduced several new techniques, primarily in abdominal surgery. He took no fees from his work at the sanitarium or for any of his surgeries. His entire personal income was from royalties from the nearly 50 books and medical treatises that he published during his long career. Dr. Kellogg wrote primarily about his principles of "biological living," constantly seeking to educate the public, as well as his peers in the medical profession, about the virtues of his health reform ideas.

Celebrated American figures who visited the sanitarium include Mary Todd Lincoln, Sojourner Truth, J. C. Penney, Montgomery Ward, Dale Carnegie, John D. Rockefeller, Thomas Edison, Booker T. Washington, Admiral Byrd, Amelia Earhart, and Professor Ivan Pavlov of Leningrad a Nobel Prize for Medicine recipient, and President of the United States, William H. Taft.

At the sanitarium, Kellogg explored various treatments for his patients, including diet reform. He encouraged a low-fat, low-protein diet with an emphasis on whole grains, fiber-rich foods, and most importantly, nuts. Kellogg also recommended a daily intake of fresh air, exercise, and the importance of hygiene. Many of the theories of John Harvey Kellogg were later published in his book, The Road to Wellness. The following quotation was the cornerstone of what was taught at the Sanitarium.

"Pure air, sunlight, abstemiousness, rest, exercise, proper diet, the use of water, trust in divine power—these are the true remedies. Every person should have a knowledge of nature's remedial agencies and how to apply them. It is essential both to understand the principles involved in the treatment of the sick and to have a practical training that will enable one rightly to use this knowledge.

The use of natural remedies requires an amount of care and effort that many are not willing to give. Nature's process of healing and up building is .gradual, and to the impatient it seems slow. The surrender of hurtful indulgences requires sacrifice. But in the end it will be found that nature, untrammeled, does her work wisely and well. Those who persevere in obedience to her laws will reap the reward in health of body and health of mind."

(12) *Ministry of Healing, pg. 127, E.G. White 1905*

It has been proven to be as successful now as it was in Dr. Kellogg's era.

The last section of this book is going to be lifestyle enhancing program that:

✓ is simple to follow,
✓ poses no extra cost,
✓ adds years to life,
✓ available to everyone.

Until now we have explored the emotional and spiritual aspects of people. In this final chapter the focus is being switched to our physical well-being taking the Temperament Theory into consideration.

A-NEW-START
Lifestyle Program Overview

A	ttitude		Learn to Accept Yourself & Understand Others **(EMOTIONAL HEALTH)**
			(PHYSICAL HEALTH)
N	utrition		Eat whole foods as unprocessed as possible including carbohydrates and healthy fats.
E	xercise		Sensible activities to provide body motion and build strength. S ensible activities to provide body motion and build strength.
W	ater	+	Water inside and out.
S	unshine		Proper limited exposure to the healthy benefits of the sun's ultra violet rays.
T	emperance		Limiting what is harmful; overeating, health damaging beverages, anger management. Omitting unhealthful practices and mood altering substances.
A	ir		Breathing deeply of fresh air daily.
R	est		Physical--Mental--Emotional Adequate rest, 7-8 hours per night.
T	rust		Trust in Divine Power

Attitude

Learning to accept yourself and understand others is a big step. It gives us a healthy attitude and understanding of others and an acceptance and appreciation of who we are as well.

Attitude deals with the emotional part of our being. The rest of this chapter will relate to our physical well-being. The study of the Four Basic Temperaments is the "A" in the A NEW START acronym. This final chapter will relate to our physical well being.

Nutrition

Simple foods, simply prepared without the use of unhealthy fats have proven to be the best diet.

Researchers documented the healthy practices of some 6,900 people in Alameda County, California and followed and reported them for 9 years and reported their findings. The study showed four eating practices to be strong predictors of good health:

1. A healthy satisfying breakfast is the best way to start the day.
2. Eating nuts regularly, at least 5 times or more per week.
3. Eating primarily whole grain breads and cereals (at least 3+servings daily).
4. Eating primarily a plant-based diet free of meat high in fat and cholesterol.
5. Drinking plenty of water daily (at least 5 to 8 glasses daily).

(13) Breslow and Belloc, Preventative Medicine Vol. 1:409-421; Vol. 2:67-81; Vol. 9:469-48

Nutrition and the temperaments...

A person's temperament has a great impact on how he deals with lifestyle changes.

 **Sanguines** are more interested in taste than temperance. They would rather not put a lot of effort into restricting anything that gives them pleasure. They need to be encouraged to plan ahead for feeling good and having good times without being denied anything that brings them pleasure. They like immediate gratification so it is important they see the benefits and pleasures of a healthy diet.

 Cholerics have their ambitious nature on their side when it comes to nutrition. They would rather work than eat so they have the advantage of burning up excess calories without concentrating on additional physical activities.

 **Melancholies** are detailed people that like to know and take care of issues before they occur. They are more self-disciplined than the other three temperaments.

 **Phlegmatics** are naturally are prone to just take life as it is rather than be proactive. Once they make up their mind to do something—it will happen. They do not need fanfare, just a desire to make a change.

Exercise

Outside and/or **Inside**

- Exercise slows down the aging process,
- strengthens the heart,
- lowers blood pressure,
- relieves stress,
- combats depression,
- preserves muscle function,
- helps maintain desirable weight,
- restores energy,
- improves sleep,
- strengthens bones.

You do not need expensive equipment or a health club membership to start. Simply walking thirty minutes a day can provide all these benefits and more. Studies have found that physical activity is consistently one of the best predictors of a long life.

A person's temperament is a big factor in the type of exercise program that will work for them. Take walking for instance. Cholerics and Sanguines would rather walk fast and probably be talking, whereas Melancholies and Phlegmatics would walk slower and talk less, if at all.

The rays of the sun provide the only natural source of vitamin D. Caution should be taken because if the skin is exposed to sunlight for long periods of time too much can cause skin cancer. *Hint:* Let the skin be exposed to the rays of the sun for fifteen minutes before applying sunscreen to get your body's daily need of Vitamin D while walking outdoors. Research is showing that there is a problem with people dying from lack of Vitamin D than with too much. Check out this website of the International Journal of Epidemiology for more information.
(14)*http://health.usnews.com/health-news/family-health/heart/articles/2008/06/23/time-in-the-sun-how-much-is-needed-for-vitamin-dprint.html (pg. 109)*

The Temperaments and Exercise

Sanguines

Sanguines are extroverts so they would enjoy activities that involve others. If they go for a walk, they would like someone else or a group of people for company. They like to go to a gym for the socialization well as the exercise. Organized sports, where they are part of a team, works well for them. If it is fun, they are more likely to continue.

Cholerics

These utilitarian, competitive people want the time spent to be useful and to be accomplishing something with their time. Taking a walk means more to them if it has a purpose such as walking to an appointment, to lose weight, to visit someone etc. They prefer to be alone so they can go at their own pace and have time to think. They also enjoy competitive sports.

Melancholies

Exercise for a melancholy would be something planned. They do not need others to motivate them. They also enjoy organized activities. They prefer the quiet activities like going for a walk, riding a bicycle or going to a gym. Routines work well for them. They are self-motivated.

Phlegmatics

Phlegmatics are low key, slow people. Their idea of exercise is watching television. They are spectators rather than participators, but if and when they exercise, it will probably be something quiet out in nature like gardening, walking a dog, fishing, or paddling a kayak.

Water

Inside & Out

Water is to the body what oil is to a car engine. It is the lubricant that makes everything else work efficiently. A drink of water is exactly what the body needs to carry out many of its life processes.

Water is the most important nutrient we can put into our bodies next to air. It is essential for life. Without water we would die in a few days. The body loses about 10-12 cups of water a day through the skin, lungs and elimination processes. Food provides two to four cups of water, leaving us about eight 8oz. glasses to drink per day.

Hint: Do not drink water with, or just prior to, eating a meal. Water dilutes the enzymes that are needed to digest the food.

Water is good for us in more ways than drinking. Water is used to keep bacteria off our skin, protecting us from germs. It cleans and refreshes our whole body in a shower or bath.

Before medications became popular, Hydrotherapy, a simple home treatment of illness and disease had proven to be as effective as or more so than medications without the ill effects medications can cause. This was one of the methods of treatment Dr. Kellogg used that gave Battle Creek Sanitarium its status as "the place to go" for health and relaxation.

Whereas it is important to get professional medical diagnosis of what the health issue is before using home remedies, there are many things we can do to help ourselves and our family. Our family saved time and money over the years by using simple home remedies. Another plus is that the immune system was strengthened to help itself fight off future invasions. There are many sources of information on how to use home remedies to relieve health related issues.

Sunlight

Sunlight is essential for life. It heats the earth and sparks the photosynthesis in plants that feed all living things.

Vitamin D is known as the "Sunshine Vitamin". It has been shown that fifteen minutes of daily exposure of the skin to the sun three times a week will provide all the Vitamin D required by the body.

Unfortunately, the same wave lengths that activate the production of Vitamin D also causes aging of the skin and skin cancer. There are times when too much of a good thing can cause problems, such as overexposure to sunlight. Sunscreen must be applied to protect the skin from too much exposure to sunlight. Allowing the direct rays of the sun for 15-20 minutes before applying sunscreen is all the time needed for the body to produce the necessary Vitamin D the body needs. The darker the skin the more time is needed before the sunscreen is applied.

14).http://health.usnews.com/health-news/family-health/heart/articles/2008/06/23/time-in-the-sun-how-much-is-needed-for-vitamin-d_print.html (pg. 109)

During the deadly TB epidemic patients with the dreaded tuberculosis were cured by having their beds taken out in the fresh air. This was discovered when the hospitals became so full with TB patients that the sickest were taken outside to protect the rest of the patients. The ones outdoors improved while the ones inside became worse.

Just as with all other good things sunlight can be damaging if not used in moderation. Overly tanning can be very damaging to the skin causing cancer. Light skinned people and redheads should have much less exposure to the sun than darker skinned people.

Welcome the sunshine into your home by letting the sunshine in. It will improve your health and give your spirit a boost.

_Temperance

Temperance encompasses more than just food. It is moderation of what is good and elimination of anything that is harmful to our wellbeing.

Avoid what is harmful: unhealthful food and beverages, health damaging lifestyles, over indulgences, mood-altering substances, worrying, and negative emotions.

Too much of a good thing can become a bad thing when your health is involved. Common sense and moderation will do more for you than any health fad or miracle food. Balance is the key to good health——we should to learn to apply it to all areas in our life.

We are what we eat.

Other areas that temperance or moderation should be considered to keep a good balance in our lives are:

Rest /Activity
Sleep/Awake
Joy/ Sorrow
Solitude/Companionship
Serious/Lighthearted
Work/Play

Air

Air is of prime importance for life to continue. A person can live for a few days without food or perhaps even without water. But it is impossible to survive even a few minutes without air.

One of the simplest ways to gain energy and clear your mind is to breathe in fresh wholesome air. When we breathe in oxygen, the air enters the lungs and dissolves in the blood. Then when we breathe out, poisonous carbon dioxide is expelled purifying the lungs. Deep breathing allows fresh air while invigorating the mind and body.

The best air to breathe is out in open space where there are trees and grass because green plants put oxygen into the atmosphere. Early morning provides fresh, pure, oxygen-rich air, which purifies the blood and body and clears the mind.

Although air pollution is everywhere we go, there needs to be some personal accountability for the quality of the air we breathe. We should have more fresh air circulating throughout our homes. Try opening the windows each day to refresh the air quality in your home.

With every beat our heart is sending blood-carrying oxygen throughout the body. Be aware not to constrict blood flow with tight clothing or bands. These items are restricting for the proper blood flow to and from the heart.

Rest

Rest gives the body time to renew itself, remove waste, repair itself and replenish energy. It restores the body's immune system, which helps to protect us from diseases. Proper rest can add years to your life. How much sleep do you need?

The National Sleep Foundation recommends:

Newborns, 0-2 months, 12-18 hrs.   School age, 5-10 years   10-11 hrs.
Infants, 3-11 months,   14-15 hrs.   Teens (10-17)years   8 ½ -9 ½ hrs.
Toddlers 1-3 years,   12-14 hrs.   Adults require   7-9 hrs.
Preschoolers, 3-5 years, 11-13hrs.

15) http://www.sleepfoundation.org/article/how-sleep-works/how-much-sleep-do-we-really-need

There are two terms relating to sleep that need to be mentioned: Melatonin and Circadian Rhythm.

Melatonin often called, the hormone of darkness, is a natural chemical our body produces which regulates our sleep. Light inhibits the release of melatonin into our system but releases it when it is dark.

Circadian rhythm is our body's internal biological clock. Nature operates on cycles such as the seasons in a year, and the rotation of the earth every 24 hours. We have daylight to be awake and darkness to sleep. There are numerous reasons why people do not sleep when it is dark. It would do well for people that sleep during daylight hours or in rooms that are not dark to darken the room as much as possible and/or wear a mask over their eyes to simulate darkness enabling the melatonin to do its job to keep their body's circadian rhythm intact.

The following are a few suggestions to getting a good night's rest.
- ✓ Have routines such as going to bed at the same time each day.
- ✓ Take a daily walk out in the sunshine whenever possible.
- ✓ Most people eat meals in the wrong order. The most substantial meal should be eaten in the morning and the lightest one in the evening. This allows the digestive system to rest at night.
- ✓ Maintain an attitude of gratitude.
- ✓ Take a warm bath or shower before going to bed.
- ✓ Put the cares of life aside and think of pleasant things.
- ✓ Be thankful for what you have.

_T_rust in Divine Power

Studies at Harvard University found that people who trust in a higher power have a strong spiritual belief system recover more quickly from illness. Meditation, prayer, and other non-medical healing activities are associated with decreased mortality from heart disease. These and other forms of spiritual activity have repeatedly been found to lower blood pressure.

- We each have a Heavenly Father that we can go to with confidence knowing that He is available for us at all times.
  (16) 1U.S.News & WORLD REPORT, June 16, 2009

- Health Prayer: Should Religion and Faith Have Roles in Medicine?

"In recent years, a growing number of rigorous studies have shown that spirituality—including prayer, meditation, and attendance at religious services—benefits health in ways that science hasn't fully explained. Among other effects, regular worship and other spiritual acts appear to lengthen life expectancy, strengthen immunity, improve the body's response to stress, and boost other measures of physical health."
(17) By Christine Larson, Posted December 22, 2008

Sad to say Battle Creek Sanitarium is no longer available. The following is contact information for people wanting to be proactive in improving their health.

Weimar Center of Health & Education
Mailing Address: PO Box 486, Weimar, CA 95736
Physical Address: 20601 West Paoli Lane, Weimar, CA 95736
Telephone: (530) 637-4111
Fax: (530-4722
Web site:https://weimar.com

esthermarywhite@gmail.com